How to Succeed in your Counselling and Psychotherapy Training

How to Succeed in your Counselling and Psychotherapy Training

Cecilia Jarvis

Mc Graw Hill

Open University Press

Open University Press
McGraw Hill
Unit 4
Foundation Park
Roxborough Way
Maidenhead
SL6 3UD

email: emea_uk_ireland@mheducation.com
world wide web: www.mheducation.co.uk

Executive Editor: Eleanor Christie
Editorial Assistant: Hannah Jones
Content Product Manager: Ali Davis

A catalogue record of this book is available from the British Library

ISBN-13: 9780335252114
ISBN-10: 0335252117
eISBN: 9780335252121

Library of Congress Cataloging-in-Publication Data
CIP data applied for

Typeset by Transforma Pvt. Ltd., Chennai, India

Praise Page

"*A much needed and long-awaited book: the author pulls together their extensive experience in training to address the key questions, anxieties and practicalities faced by those considering or embarking on a career in the psychological therapies' professions. From questioning one's underlying motivations through choosing a course, entering clinical placement, to seeking professional accreditation, this book offers guidance and lived-experience accounts of what it's like to be a trainee therapist in today's provision of psychological wellbeing services. An important read for all wishing to succeed in their training.*"

Professor John Nuttall, Regent's University London and
Chair of West London Centre for Counselling, UK

"*This is an eminently useful and accessible book for anyone considering embarking on counselling and psychotherapy training. It gives a broad perspective on the flow of training, from choosing a course, to giving more detailed guidance on placements, supervision and assessment. The language is direct and clear throughout and there are useful reflective exercises. I can recommend it to anyone considering training, or at the beginning part of their journey.*"

Dr Biljana van Rijn, Metanoia Institute, UK

"*In this well written, up to date comprehensive book, Cecilia Jarvis covers a vast range of practical, ethical and clinical issues to guide students every step of the way through their counselling and psychotherapy training. It is thorough, clearly structured, interesting and an easy to read handbook. I enjoyed reading it and will be recommending it.*"

Siobhán McGee, Director & Tutor, Karuna Institute, UK

"*'How to Succeed in your Counselling and Psychotherapy Training' is a unique and useful guide, walking counselling and psychotherapy trainees through from the beginning of their training and clinical practice to their post-qualifying year. Jarvis is well-positioned to map this journey as a highly experienced and esteemed trainer, practitioner, and supervisor. The book addresses a wide range of topics in a lucid and accessible way, from practicalities, such as choosing a course, to complex processes, such as engaging in clinical supervision and working with the therapeutic relationship. It offers orientation, advice, clarifications of key areas, and support for self-reflection. The book is a gem!*"

Maya Mukamel, PhD, Director of Studies,
The Integrative Psychotherapy Programme, Metanoia Institute

"This beautifully structured manual serves as a companion to navigating the complex and multi-layered journey of a therapy training. As well as very grounded, practical information, this book contains more subtle tips and gems of wisdom which will greatly help to alleviate the many and varied anxieties of new trainees. The contents have been gained at the coalface of teaching and reflect the wealth of experience as a counselling tutor that Cecilia has accumulated in close to 30 years in the role. It adds an invaluable contribution to any reading list for Counselling and Psychotherapy trainings."

Sue Healey BACP Accredited Counsellor, Counselling Tutor

Contents

Preface

Having been involved in the training of counsellors and psychotherapists in different capacities for a very long time, I draw here on the experiences of what new and developing trainees go through on their training journey. This book is primarily written for those people who have just started a professional clinical training in counselling or psychotherapy or those considering embarking on one. Its aim is to clarify what happens in the different parts of what constitutes a clinical training – the work in the training room, the work in the clinical placement, what happens in supervision and the ongoing journey of knowing oneself. Above all it signals how we listen and respond to our clients in a therapeutic relationship.

The first six chapters consider very practical elements of the training journey and the challenges surrounding them. The remaining chapters are focused on building a robust therapeutic presence and how to work within the therapeutic relationship. Readers can dip in and out of chapters, depending on their current needs or interests.

Throughout the book there are self-reflection exercises, and in many places the voices of trainees who have generously shared their experience of the training journey.

Use of language

I have written Chapters 1 and 10 more directly to the reader. The other chapters are more formally written.

I also use the generic term therapist to mean both counsellor and psychotherapist, as both face many similar challenges in these early clinical years. In places I have used 'new trainee' or 'new therapist' to give emphasis to the very early days of starting out in placement. In all chapters relating to work in the placement I use the term therapist.

Acknowledgements

Many people – friends and colleagues and students – have encouraged and supported the creation of this book, for which I am very grateful.

There have been my students past and present who have contributed ideas or their own experiences of being in training. They include Sarah Carr, Joe Carreiro, Rebecca Chapman, Mark Davies, Helen Lavelle, Zornitsa Litova, Kristen McCarthy, Heather Nunn, Clare Parfitt, Kristin Ramsay, Rachel Remedios and Eva Tyler. With special thanks to year 2 (2021–2) who contributed individually and collectively. They are Han Bestwick, Phil Cairns, Keeley Dann, Tom Edwards, Nicola Foster, Sarah Fysh, Sally Hartley, Elif Köklü, Karen Lynch, Elyssa McKeown, Rehana Mohamedali, Jennie O'Connor, Justin Pryce, Tania Raymond, Lucie Regent, Nuria Robinson, Natalie Salmon, Jacqueline Shearman and Joanne Williams.

To my colleagues who contributed to the Professional Diploma in Integrative Counselling, in particular Penny Cloutte, who co-founded the above course with me. Also Julia Wright, Dragana Djukic, Sophia Prevezanou and more recently Linda Barrett, Lorna Fulton and Susan Healey, and all the in-house supervisors on the course.

To my friend and colleague Eva Bailey who read most of the manuscript and made valuable contributions to it, to my supervisor Katherine Murphy for her robust thinking over the years, and to Peter Tite who did an enormous job in doing the first proofreading of the various chapters.

To my husband an enormous thanks for his undying support and practical help in the challenging moments.

Cecilia Jarvis

1 Embarking on training in counselling and psychotherapy

It is a huge decision to enter a counsellor or psychotherapy training programme. The interest in working with people will have been brewing for years, if not decades, but will have become a definite professional and personal objective at some point. This creates the necessary curiosity to think more deeply about why you want to train as a therapist and the energy to research what is available and appropriate for you in the training world. In my former profession as a teacher of history, a pivotal moment came when I was teaching an exam class about the rise of Fascism and I thought 'I can't do this job for the next 30 years.' I believe we do need to know about history so that we have a wider perspective on the world, but for me it felt too cognitive. What I had liked as a teacher was helping my pupils to gain in confidence and overcome difficulties that made the learning process challenging to them.

It's good to start by talking to someone who knows about training or who has done counselling or psychotherapy training themselves. I was fortunate at that time to meet a colleague's friend who was a trained therapist. This gave me a better flavour of what training entails. Being able to go to an open day at a training organization or doing a short taster day or course gives you personal experience of being in a training organization. It will give you the 'feel' of the organization, which is important to notice and see if you actually like it. This is one of the 'soft' factors in making your choice.

Motivation for embarking on a therapeutic training

As well as considering practical issues you need to examine your motives for wanting to do counselling or psychotherapy training. In application forms and at interviews you will be asked about why you want to train as a therapist. All candidates have both known and unknown reasons and motivations. The seeds of these will have been sown in early experiences in childhood and will have been influenced by events, responses and experiences that have come from the culture in which you grew up as a teenager and adult.

Many conscious motives for wanting to help others come from benevolent and altruistic attitudes. Sussman (1992: 13) writes: 'For some it may be an expression of compassion, or moral duty, or perhaps guilt.' There is also the pleasure of listening to another, the sense of feeling helpful to society, the joy of helping another to uncover the mystery of their life story, the experience of doing work that is predominantly about human contact. Potential therapists also have unconscious motives for wanting to train. Sussman's extensive review of the literature suggests: 'Those individuals who choose to become therapists typically manifest significant psychological conflicts of their own' (Sussman 1992: 239). These internal conflicts may centre around issues of identity and self-esteem – both personal and professional – intimacy and separation, how power is held, how to relate to vulnerability, and an unconscious motivation to heal other aspects of personal and intergenerational trauma. In my own journey into training I was clear about my conscious motivation – I liked helping people, but the way in which I was doing it was not the best way for me. I also had group therapy at university which was deeply significant for me, so I was confident about therapy being valuable and transformative. However I didn't quite realize the depth of my unconscious motivation for training when I applied for a training place, but I was happy to know that I would be in therapy again.

What is important in the above is the potential therapist's attitude to be willing to explore their hidden motivations. The training journey provides many opportunities for exploration and development of parts of our wounded self so that we know ourselves better. I am still on this journey, refining my understanding of the deeper meanings for me doing this work.

Choosing a course

As the momentum grows in you to train you will need to do research about training programmes and courses and start to consider choices. The key elements in making your decision are about what kind of professional qualification you want, what therapeutic modality fits you best and what are the practical implications of doing the course? If the above do not fit well with you there will be a tension throughout your training experience.

What is clinical training?

In order to work professionally as a counsellor or psychotherapist you will do what is known as clinical training. That means that the course will require you to have practical experience working with clients under supervision whilst you are in training. This is the element that ties in most closely with your motivation for embarking on a therapeutic training in the first place – the pleasure derived from listening to another human being's story. However there are other choices you will need to make when you consider which course is best for you. The main choices you need to make are: what qualification do you want to do and where do you want to do it?

Types of training organizations

Counselling and psychotherapy training is provided by a wide variety of training organizations such as private training organizations, further education (FE) or adult education institutes, and higher education (HE) (i.e. in universities). The qualifications range from diplomas (advanced or postgraduate) to degrees.

The differences between counselling and psychotherapy training

As a rule of thumb, the differences between counselling training and psychotherapy training are that counselling training:

- is shorter – about three years overall
- does not always insist on weekly personal therapy – courses vary
- uses the title 'counselling' in the qualification it offers
- requires a minimum of 100 hours of clinical practice at the point of qualification.

In the broadest terms psychotherapy training:

- is longer – at least four taught years, and probably five years overall
- insists on weekly therapy during the training years
- uses the title 'psychotherapy' in the qualification it offers
- requires a minimum of 450 hours of clinical practice at the point of qualification.

All of the above have major implications for you and your life for at least three to five years, and should be considered very carefully.

Course structure

Professional training programmes have different course structures and are of different lengths. Typically, counsellor training takes place over three years. It may consist of a foundation year or stand-alone Level 3 counselling skills training plus a two-year diploma (at least Level 4) or postgraduate diploma (PGDip), or alternatively a diploma or PGDip training programme taught over three continuous years.

Psychotherapy training is generally four to five years in duration. It may consist of a three-year counsellor training course with an additional two years of training to fulfil the requirements for a psychotherapy qualification. This in itself is contentious and some people will argue that you either start training as a counsellor or as a psychotherapist, and that you can't start on one road and change track onto the other. Alternatively, from the start you can do a four- or five-year psychotherapy training course.

Changing training organizations

What you end up choosing as best for your circumstances has professional and personal implications. Some people do their foundation year/Level 3 training and then decide on a change of training organization. A common reason is that a foundation course/Level 3 gives a broad overview of the different therapeutic modalities, and you find that the approach you are most interested in is not the one offered by your present training organization.

The other big point of change may come after qualifying as a counsellor, if you wish to pursue further study. Some people like to take the long view and wish to train as a psychotherapist or counsellor in one particular organization. Others might welcome a change after three years and want to move to another training organization. Mixing and matching is not always easy, and training organizations may require applicants to do specific training or evidence specific learning before they are eligible for that particular course. The most common reason to change is that a person wants to enhance a professional counsellor qualification into either a degree or psychotherapy qualification and will have to do this through another training organization. The only thing that is certain is that training organizations have different entry requirements at each level, so you need to check them out carefully before applying.

Is a degree important?

To work professionally as a counsellor or psychotherapist there is no requirement that you have an academic degree in the subject. Some training programmes do offer a degree as the qualification, e.g. a BA or MA in Counselling or a Master's in Psychotherapy. So one question for you is: how much does a degree matter to you? Many well-established and reputable counselling and psychotherapy training courses do not offer a degree with the clinical qualification, or they offer the degree as an additional option.

Training in the time of Coronavirus and afterwards

At the time of writing (2022) there has been a major change in the training world in that before the first Coronavirus lockdown of March 2020 most training in the UK was done in the classroom. As a response to the pandemic many training courses successfully adapted to offering temporary online training. As we come out of this period, there is an emerging area across the counselling and psychotherapy profession which is giving attention to the paradigm shift that the professions have experienced. The professional bodies, the awarding bodies (e.g. examination boards and universities) and training organizations will continue to consider the requirements of training post-pandemic. Two main aspects of this are: how much training will be delivered in the room and how much will be delivered online, and what proportion of clinical hours will be in the room and how much can be accrued online. 'Blended' training means there will be both online and in-the-classroom components. There is also 'hybrid learning' which consists of in-the-classroom learning with students joining online at the same time. At the moment there are no plans for any entirely online training.

The main advantage of online training is that time and money on travel is not needed. Also training will be more accessible to people who do not live near, or find it difficult to travel to the organization, hence widening access for the course.

However the training day online can feel very long and tiring, causing concentration to lapse. This is because of having to sit far more still when working online than sitting in the classroom. We are also looking at many predominantly still faces on screen. Something gets a bit frozen. Another disadvantage I hear about from my students is the lack of contact with their peers. What is missing is the 'soft' contact of having tea together, taking a break outside near the college premises, walking to catch public transport together, which have all been sorely missed. Online 'cafe' time is valuable but is not quite the same as in-the-room, in-the-flesh presence and contact with another human being. Students also like getting out of their home to study. This has a different feel to learning at home and can feel like a breath of fresh air during the week. What you need to consider is how much online training, or what balance of classroom/online training, will be good for you. This might be a big determining factor in choosing a training course. Course brochures and an organization's public facing websites will need to clearly set out how much classroom/online training will be in their course structures.

The role of professional bodies in relation to accreditation of courses

Professional bodies such as the British Association for Counselling and Psychotherapy (BACP) and the UK Council for Psychotherapy (UKCP) have many functions in relation to the profession and its wider context. The work of these professional bodies includes setting standards of working practice by providing an ethical framework or code of practice for their members to adhere to and work with. In relation to this they also provide a forum which members of the public who feel they have not received good service from a qualified therapist can use to bring their concern and/or complaints to the professional body for scrutiny.

In regard to training, the above professional organizations can accredit a training course. Accreditation of a course means that the course the training organization offers has been approved as meeting the standard for counselling or psychotherapy training. If this accreditation is given, the course can say it is a BACP or UKCP accredited course. (These descriptors refer to the status of a course, not an individual therapist.)

So into the above mix of factors in your decision-making can be added the status of the course provided by a training organization. It is important to note that at this time training organizations are not obliged to put their courses forward for accreditation or validation by the above professional bodies. This process is costly and time-consuming for trainers, and the training organization may not do this.

The SCoPEd Framework

At the moment there is a vast range of training available, from short-term training (e.g. 6–12 weeks' training in bereavement support work), to stand-alone basic skills training (e.g. at Level 3), up to professional training courses in counselling and psychotherapy (from Levels 4 to 7). It is often difficult for a member of the public to understand how trained and qualified any individual therapist is and to what professional body the therapist belongs. Additionally, potential mental health employers may be unclear about what a therapist's level of training and qualifications means. The SCoPEd project was formed to bring clarity and transparency about standards in training, and the experience requirements of therapists.

The SCoPEd Framework (2022) has been the work of several professional bodies: Association of Christian Counsellors (ACC), British Association for Counselling and Psychotherapy (BACP), British Psychoanalytic Council (BPC), Human Givens Institute (HGI), National Counselling Society (NSC) and the UK Council for Psychotherapy (UKCP). The Framework (2022: 3) clarifies 'the core training, practice and competence requirements for counsellors and psychotherapists working with adults'. It is a detailed document which sets out 'the training and practice requirements associated with different entry and progression points for the profession, and the core competencies required for safe and ethical practice for counsellors and psychotherapists' (SCoPEd Framework 2022: 5).

In brief, the Framework defines training, practice and competency in three columns. These columns are not rigid and therapists will be able to move between columns as they gain more experience and competency.

For entry to column A, there will need to be at least two years' core training or experience, 300–400 training hours and a minimum of 100 hours of client practice, with an average 1.5 hours' supervision per month.

For entry to column B, there will need to be at least three years' core training with 450 training hours (at Levels 4 to 7) and 450 hours of client practice (including clinical hours gained after qualifying as a counsellor), with a minimum of 1.5 hours, supervision per month.

For column C, there will be a core training of four years with a minimum of 500 training hours and training of at least Level 7, with 450 client hours gained during training.

There are also other requirements for entry to the different columns regarding the amount of personal therapy, the ratio of supervision to client work and a mental health familiarization placement.

What therapeutic orientation do I choose?

This can be a very difficult decision to make. For your best interests you need to do some research around this – at the very least you should go to an introductory course to get a feel for what is on offer. Bear in mind that there are several main schools of counselling and psychotherapy in the UK at the moment. All of them have variations and different emphases within them, but here are the 'broad churches' or therapeutic modalities:

- Behavioural and cognitive schools, which focus on helping the person to remove unhelpful thoughts and behaviours.
- Psychodynamic schools, which focus on how we relate to ourselves and others unconsciously and how elements in the present have been shaped by our past.
- Humanistic and existential schools, which pay most attention to the 'now' in the therapy room and the interplay of the therapeutic relationship.
- Integrative models, which bring together at least two theoretical models in theory and practice.
- Transpersonal schools, which include the concept that the spiritual dimension of life can be a healing force.
- Body psychotherapies, which work predominantly through the client's body awareness.

Unless you are very clear that you want to follow a particular orientation, you face a journey, which will not always be clear-cut or straight, into training. Steps on this journey could include:

- simple curiosity in signing up for a short course in a particular therapeutic modality
- reading a book or article about a theorist or therapeutic journey that piques your interest
- hearing from a friend or colleague about a training programme or organization which sounds interesting.

After you have taken some initial steps of exploration into training, the more serious decision about signing up to a longer training course can be challenging. It is important that you consider and weigh up your heartfelt emotional response and the practical factors which make a particular course appealing or otherwise.

Heartfelt responses centre around the best fit for you of:

- the key elements of the training model and how the model sits with your beliefs about people, the world and what creates healing
- how the organization feels to you – i.e. the vibe you get from the organization
- the teaching style of the trainers (if you have had a taste of it)
- the practical elements of the training and if they fit with where you are in your life at that point
- the real and genuine sense of the timing being right for you at this juncture in your life.

Practical implications

Training demands time, energy and money. So try to be as clear as possible about the requirements when you are considering what training to choose.

Time

Regarding time, there are the stated training hours spent in the classroom, which should be clear from the course's literature – e.g. a whole day's training, weekend training, or a combination of the two.

In addition there is the time spent in a clinical placement:

- Induction training and any ongoing training provided by the agency.
- The actual time seeing the clients – usually two to three hours per week.
- Supervision time in the placement – this can vary enormously. Some placements are able to provide supervision on the day you see clients, while others ask you to attend on a different day. Some placements do not provide supervision! In this case you (the trainee) may incur additional costs for private supervision if your training organization requires it.

In addition there is the time for attending personal therapy – how much does your course require as mandatory? There may be supervision outside of training time if this is not provided by the placement or the training organization. All of these components and activities consume several hours a week, not including travel time. A prospective trainee may have calculated some of these elements before applying for training, but its effects will be felt once they actually start!

It is crucial to make agreements with employers about what time you might need to take off for your training. One colleague of mine used up all their annual leave in order to fit in his training. Practically this may be possible, but you need to consider how this might affect your own well-being in terms of increased stress and feeling tired.

More difficult to ascertain is the psychological time needed – the thinking space in your head, to read, write, think about clients, ponder on what you have learned in supervision, to reflect on yourself after personal therapy. Some of these are digested and processed unconsciously as the trainee goes along. However, if the trainee is so stressed by the demands of the course, and perhaps their personal life, they can start operating in firefighting mode rather than reflecting on what is happening inside and outside of themselves. Downtime is needed to mull over all the different elements of training. The trainee therapist might survive, but not thrive and develop, if they have a high level of stress in their system. Therapeutic training makes demands on the participant in different ways from any predominantly academic training because you, the trainee, need to be personally involved in all aspects of the learning and ensuing processes. It doesn't just happen in your head! In therapeutic training the personal and the professional are closely connected and mutually influential. So ask yourself, 'is this the right time in my life to embark on training?'

Energy and resources

All of the above will make demands on the trainee's energy and personal resources. Having carved out of your life the calculated time needed to do the course, how do you ensure that you have the energy to do everything? One aspect that is rarely considered is who in the trainee's life, outside of the peer training group, can offer psychological support and perhaps practical assistance during the period of training? It is very difficult to keep going in the challenging times of training if significant others are anti the training and non-supportive. You will need resources and resilience to get through all the training. If you are over-stretched it is probably not the right time to embark on it.

Money

Training is expensive. Training organizations charge different fees and there will be other costs associated with the programme. At the time of writing (2022), students and trainees may be able to apply for a government loan called the Advanced Learner Loan if they are doing a Level 3, 4, 5 or 6 course. But be aware that not all training organizations are linked to this scheme. The loan covers or partly covers the fees for the course and is paid directly to the training organization, not the trainee. It is repayable after the end of the training. However, it does not cover all the costs, so be clear about what you will have to budget for apart from the fees for the course itself. The main additional costs are likely to centre on the fees for personal therapy and supervision (if not included in the course and not provided by the placement), books, membership of professional organizations, examination fees, registration fees and equipment such as digital recorders. All of these costs may come on top of a salary reduction if you have reduced your working hours to fit in the demands of the course.

Trainee voice – choosing a course

- *Compare costs of training programmes before signing up; the formal course fees and the costs of therapy – depending on the requirement of the course.*
- *Are there costs for supervision?*
- *Also, what life costs will be required, such as childcare arrangements, travel.*
- *Find out which courses are funded by the Advanced Learner Loan.*

Self-reflection

- *Make a list of 'heart' factors and a list of 'head' practicalities about what is important to you in a training course.*
- *Read the lists slowly to yourself – let them sink in.*
- *Allow yourself to imagine putting the lists on an old-fashioned set of balance scales to be weighed.*
- *What do you see as you look at the scales? Try not to censor.*

- *Allow yourself to draw how the scales look and feel to you.*
- *What do you see? What seems to be most important?*

  You may wish to do this a couple of times or to select specific elements of your dilemma about courses – e.g. weighing up time commitments with what feels the closest fit to your philosophy.

Sometimes there is not a straightforward, uncomplicated answer, in which case it is important to take time with your decision-making until you get clearer. No-one fully knows if the course will absolutely suit them until they are actually doing the training.

Applications and interviews

Writing a good application is crucially important if a training course is in demand. Take time to read the questions on the application form and to answer them as reflectively as you can. Having other relevant experience, e.g. as a Samaritan or work in the caring professions, is important to include. If you are not confident in your writing, ask a friend or a colleague to read the application form and give you some feedback on it. You will need to provide the certificates for any previous qualifications you have gained. You will also be asked to give the name of at least one referee who could support your application. Doing a serious application takes time.

No course for a professional qualification (diploma/Level 4 and above) will offer you a place without an interview. The trainers need to meet you and get a sense of who you are as a person. The interview may be individual or in a group, or both. You may be asked to bring a piece of work which you completed on a foundation training course for the trainers to read. They will request references so as to have a fuller picture of who you are.

Prepare for an interview and settle yourself before meeting the trainers. Knowing what you bring as a person and what you can bring to the profession is critical.

Offers of a training place

Once you have received an offer of a training place, be prepared for paperwork to follow. Make sure you complete all the paperwork by the given date or you might lose your place on the course. Contact the tutors or course administrator if you have some difficulties with these administrative procedures.

If you did not receive a place you may be put on a waiting list. Sometimes trainers advise an applicant to do some personal development work or therapy and to reapply in the future.

Getting started and settling in

Once you have received an offer and completed all the admin surrounding the training contract, you will be ready to meet your training group and embark upon the training for a new professional life. The main elements at the start of training consist of getting to know more about the course and becoming a member of your training group. In addition you will need to find a therapist (if you are not already in therapy) and you will need to start researching for a clinical placement.

The first day or two of training are usually an induction to the course which sets out in greater detail the course structure and requirements, and what is expected of you. There will also be a discussion of the group's working agreement or contract, which will include the parameters of confidentiality in the group. This is very important to establish at the outset because of the nature of therapeutic training, which involves personal disclosures. Trainees need to know what the boundaries are. I am not suggesting that the group contract is set in stone at this point. What is needed is an initial agreement that can be reviewed and renegotiated in the future if necessary.

Group dynamics at the start

There are always group dynamics in training – some are very subtle and some are more obvious. Initially the dynamics of inclusion and exclusion can play out strongly, especially if someone joins an already established group or there is a subgroup of students, within the larger group, who have previously trained together. Thinking about how you can include yourself in the group and respond to invitations to participate in the group indicate something about your own personality and interpersonal processes. It is crucial that you build working relationships in your training group, as your peers and their input will be invaluable for your learning.

Personal therapy

Courses have different requirements for personal therapy. Most courses want the trainee to be in therapy by the start of the training. Some courses have a list of 'training therapists' whom the students will work with. This is to ensure compatibility between what is taught on the training and how the 'training therapist' works. Other courses leave it up to the trainee to find a therapist, and some courses offer general guidelines about who to work with. Another variable is the requirement for the frequency and duration of therapy. For psychotherapy training it will be at least weekly therapy over the course of the training period. This usually means 40 therapy sessions per training year. Counsellor training programmes vary in their requirements, from about ten sessions to courses that want their trainees to be in weekly therapy.

Going into therapy can feel very daunting if you have never experienced it before. It is probably beneficial in the long term to make appointments to meet with at least a couple of therapists to see how you feel with them. Also be practical and check the therapist's availability when arranging an appointment with a potential therapist; if, for example, you can only have an evening appointment or see them on a particular day, find out if the therapist has suitable availability. It can be costly to meet with a potential therapist – you may think they are wonderful, only to find out that they only have 2pm on a Tuesday afternoon free, which you cannot do. But consider if you might prefer to telephone the potential therapist and hear their voice rather than making the appointment online.

Personal therapy is a huge investment emotionally, financially and in terms of a time commitment. It is often the element in training that supports, contains and challenges the trainee so that they can truly extend themselves. It offers the opportunity to look at hidden aspects of ourselves, recognize our repeating patterns, acknowledge our unmet needs, and also find strengths and resources inside ourselves.

Trainee voice – finding a therapist

'That's a tough one because it involves money and logistics so the end decision may be influenced by those factors. A trainee can start with recommendations or using the BACP platform. The key for me was following the advice from the tutors and looking at my personal therapy as an investment rather than another box to tick. Having the right attitude to personal therapy is what I think will help a trainee know if they get what they need from their therapist and challenge their therapist if they don't. Also, if their sessions feel more like a friendly chat, probably they need to move on to another therapist. If at the end of the session the trainee doesn't feel they have got what they needed from their counsellor, they should be able to say it and if it can't be worked out, move on.'

Getting ready to apply for a clinical placement

All trainees begin their clinical work under the aegis of an organization that offers a clinical placement, e.g. a bereavement agency, a local counselling or psychotherapy charity, a substance recovery agency, a school or sixth-form college service or university service. This is because the trainee needs to be held in a supportive system. A new trainee does not have the experience to assess who is suitable to take on as a client and may not have the appropriate resources such as a practice room to work in. There is also the aspect of being part of a team and a larger whole, which can be supportive when you start clinical work. Private practice is very different, and training organizations will not allow new trainees to take private clients.

Placements post-Covid-19

Since the Covid-19 pandemic the way placements offer their services has rapidly changed. Prior to this, most placements offered clinical work predominantly in the room. It will become clear over the next few years how placements will continue to provide their services. Some have moved to an online service or a partial online service, whilst others have decided to maintain in-the-room services as crucial to their founding principles. There will always be clients who benefit most from being in the presence of another human being. What you need to be clear about from your training organization is the *percentage* of the clinical hours for the qualification you are doing that you are allowed to gather, if you work online. Also, what specific training you will need to do to be deemed competent to work remotely or online. Some of this may be provided by your training organization or they may signpost you to other appropriate training. These will be important factors in determining where to apply for a placement.

Readiness to apply

Clinical placements do not commence during the foundation training year or on a Level 3 course – these are the preclinical or classroom training periods. Once you have completed this year it is advisable to begin the search for a suitable placement, which you will begin in your next year. If you find a placement that you are interested in, make some general enquiries about when and how often they recruit. Some do this at set points in the year whilst others have a rolling recruitment procedure. This research takes time and patience and is an important investment in your development as a therapist. Your training organization may have a list of placements that their trainees have worked in, and looking at this is a good start. However, it is the individual trainee's responsibility to engage with this task.

Inherent in the above is the fact that your training organization has given you the green light to start clinical work. This in itself is a complex process both practically and psychologically. The training organization will have input into this – e.g. they will have agreed that your skills have reached a certain level, and that you have fulfilled other requirements such as being in your own therapy or have found a supervisor for the work (if they do not provide in-house supervision). Some trainers want to see you in action in a skills session before they agree that you are ready to start clinical work, whereas others take the view that if you have successfully completed a foundation year or Level 3 training, then these are enough to prove you have the basic competency to commence clinical work. They may also have set a time by which you need to start seeing clients.

Harder to determine are your own feelings of readiness. You may think you should feel ready or you may feel competitive with your peers if they have already started working with clients. Reflection with your own therapist and discussion with your course tutor may help you to see if you are psychologically ready to begin this clinical work. Unconscious fears about failing, not being good enough or needing to be perfect from the start, can leave indelible marks on you which have an impact on how you go about seeking a placement position and actually getting one.

Self-reflection

- How ready do I feel to commence clinical work?
- What are my reservations about starting – even if these seem to be tiny ones? Name them and think about them.
- What client group do I want to work with and why? Allow yourself to consider heart and head responses to this.
- What are the attributes and life experience I can bring to working with this group?
- Make some lists of the above and hold the lists in your hands whilst having a sense that you are not an empty vessel. What do you notice?

Although there is a tremendous need for therapy provision it can be very difficult to actually find a placement. This often causes trainees to panic and think they should take whatever they might be offered.

Another way to start is to honestly consider what groups of people you want to work with and what groups of people are not right for you at this time. Thinking you can work with anyone is overconfident and ultimately unrealistic. Trainees who have had knowledge of and experience of supportive working in a specific field, e.g. substance abuse or bereavement, might wish to consider whether a fresh start with a new client group could be beneficial. The previous experience is not wasted and can be noted in application forms.

Also consider the following:

- Travelling to a particular agency, e.g. how much time and energy will it take?
- Can you work online with this agency?
- Is online work allowed by your training organization?
- Does the agency offer evening or weekend spaces if you need this?
- Is supervision included at the agency – if not, who pays for it?
- Will the agency put you on their insurance scheme or do you have to buy your own personal professional indemnity insurance?
- Does the agency require you to have a certain number of clinical hours' experience in order to be eligible to apply, or do they want you to be at a particular stage in training?
- Does your training organization make any stipulations about the kind of work and therefore placement that you should or should not be involved with at this stage of your training – e.g. concerning time-limited or longer-term work?

Applications and interviews

It is the responsibility of the trainee to make the application to a placement. It is well worth spending some time on this (just like with your application for a training place) as placements are very oversubscribed for places. Be persistent even when it feels nothing is happening or going to happen. One of my former students became somewhat despondent having sent over 20 applications without being invited to a single interview. Then he was invited to several interviews and was offered three placements. He aptly said 'It's just like waiting for buses'. Be clear about what that particular placement is offering and consider what you could bring to it. This doesn't mean you have to have prior skills or experience about the clients who use it. However, it does mean that you have to show your interest in that client group and what you could offer them.

Having completed the application form and sent it off it is useful to make a follow-up phone call or email to check that it has been received and to enquire when you might know if you have been selected for interview. Then you can prepare yourself for an interview.

For the interview reread your application form. Think again about why you would like to work at that particular placement and what you can bring to it. You will need to sell yourself!

Trainee voice – getting a placement

'I was really nervous about the application and interview process and a friend reminded me that I am offering something to the agency as well – to work for them for free with all the skills I've learned. Thinking about what I had to offer helped me feel more confident for the interview.'

'When looking for a placement, I was a bit disheartened not to get my first or second choice, but the third option has worked out very well indeed. I feel well supported and valued.'

The interview itself can take many forms. There are individual interviews where you would meet with the counselling manager or coordinator. Sometimes applicants take part in a group interview with discussion and exercises. There are interviews which involve discussion about a case to see how you are thinking about a potential client. Some of the group interviews involve a short skills session or role-play scenario so that your skills can be observed. A couple of students have had to provide a recording of a skills practice session with a commentary on the work before the actual interview.

On the day of the interview prepare and calm yourself, reaffirming what you can offer the agency at this point. Find a sense of your own self that you want to show to the interviewers. On a practical level, make sure you get to the interview ahead of time. Last-minute rushing creates anxiety and it doesn't look good if you arrive late!

Accepting a placement

Due to the competition over gaining a placement, most trainees are so delighted they have received an offer that they take it. However, it is also worth considering – even briefly – if you want this placement.

You will have got a sense of the agency from having been to the interview. If you have any reservations it is very important that you give them attention. Just as the interviewers will have picked up something about you at the interview, you will have gained some sense of the atmosphere of the agency – its structure, its administration and its people. It is very tempting to take the offer even if you have some doubts, so talk to someone, preferably your tutor, about your reservations. Consider whether it is your anxiety about actually starting clinical work or something about the placement that doesn't feel or seem right to you. Your training organization will also need to confirm whether the placement is suitable or not, so discuss this with your tutor.

When you accept a placement, there is the inevitable paperwork which goes with it – see Chapter 2 for more on this.

Off the starting blocks

Once these procedures have been completed you will be ready to start what you set out to do on the journey in the first place: the desire to alleviate suffering in another through your work as a therapist. People enter training programmes with a lot of hope and volumes of good intentions to help others. These motivations provide the necessary positive energy to get going on the demanding elements of what the training requires. It is really difficult to be fully aware just how demanding doing therapeutic training is going to be. The initial delight of receiving the offer of a training place, having your induction into the training course and meeting your tutors and peers creates vital positive energy for embarking on the course.

At some point the demands of the training begin to sink in. However, don't give up: just be as realistic as possible and be prepared to make adaptations to your pace and your training/life balance. It is critical that the seed which was planted with so much enthusiasm at the start of training is nurtured and fed as you go along; otherwise there is a danger that it will not flourish because you are too exhausted to be able to invest energy in the training and in yourself. This consideration is both a personal one for the well-being of the trainee but also an ethical one in terms of the trainee's ability to be fit to practise. It is also valuable to allow yourself to reassess the impact of the training on you and the significant people in your life. They may feel that you have little energy for them because the demands of the training are so consuming. These personal dynamics need to be noticed and thought about.

Beginning training can feel like one of the most significant decisions you have taken in your life. For many people the work becomes imbued with the sense of a deep soul journey and meaningfulness. Come back to this deep intuitive sense of the journey when the demands and struggles of being in training seem challenging. Hold this light of deeper purpose within yourself.

2 Starting work in a clinical placement

It has probably taken quite a bit of hard work to obtain a clinical placement, so getting started in the placement can feel both exciting and daunting. Working with clients in a clinical placement is deeply significant, both psychologically and practically. The new trainee is taking a step away from the familiar base of the training organization, and engaging with a client in a real context – not the skills lab or fishbowl experience of the training room. Above all, this is the first step into practising in a new profession. This shift of context is deeply laden with meaning as well as being the arena for new practical learning. Professionally and personally it's like wearing a pair of new shoes for the first time – there is the experience of the shoes, how they fit, and the new identity that comes with wearing them.

The meeting with the first client is particularly symbolic. A threshold is crossed in this session. Hence there can be a lot of anxiety about this first meeting with a client, which usually continues for a while into the early sessions. This is perfectly normal. Trainers would be concerned if trainees had no anxiety about this situation. I remember a student talking in the classroom about meeting her first client later in the week, looking absolutely terrified. When she returned the next week she said nothing about her experience. There was still an air of anxiety about her. After a few weeks she came to ask me something about another issue and I casually asked her how she was doing in the placement. She beamed as she told me she had done ten hours of client work and was loving it. I never had any doubt about her ability to survive the first session, then to learn and progress.

Knowing about how the placement works helps to allay some of the normal trepidation about beginning clinical work. Engaging well in induction sessions and taking time to prepare before meeting clients also helps to settle some of the anxious feelings.

Induction and procedures

Before they meet a client the placement will have taken their new trainees through its induction session(s), which clarify the placement's administrative policies and procedures. The main components of induction will include:

- confidentiality issues
- practical administrative procedures
- support and requirements as a member of the team
- the legal requirements of the agency.

Confidentiality issues

The placement needs to be clear about the following:

1 The confidentiality agreement between therapist and client – what this entails and how confidentiality is maintained within the agency, including in supervision, and the circumstances under which it may be broken.

2 How the communication links work within the agency, and what that means in terms of confidentiality. Initially, client data is generally administered by the placement staff. However, once a client has been referred, the therapist needs to be aware of their responsibilities around client information. These centre around confidential client data such as the client's name and address, date of birth and phone number. If the therapist is allowed to use their own mobile phone for client contact they will need to register with the Information Commissioner's Office (ICO) as they will be regarded as a data handler. Some placements provide their therapists with a simple mobile for use, but some therapists decide to buy their own separate mobile for this clinical work as this creates a clear separation between their professional and personal contacts. In some placements all contact goes through the office so the therapist is not using their own mobile. The drawback with this is that messages do not always get to the therapist promptly, but the therapist's boundaries are more protected by this system of contact.

3 How to keep client records. This is usually done on the agency computer system with password protection, or handwritten notes in a safe and confidential filing system. The agency will indicate how brief or full the client notes need to be. Also, the placement needs to make you aware of their procedures for how a client may be able to access their notes.

4 Confidentiality in supervision. It is likely that the placement supervisor will advise how they want the therapist to present a client, usually either with an initial, a first name (not necessarily the real name) or in some cases a number. Also, what is the policy if the therapist thinks they recognize a client being presented in a group supervision setting (if this is provided).

Practical administrative procedures

Some placements provide a handbook for their therapists containing their procedural systems and forms. It should clarify:

1 The cancellation and non-attendance procedures – in particular, how much notice the client needs to give in order to cancel, and whether fees are payable when there is a cancellation. What happens when a client doesn't attend several sessions – what is the policy? Is the client allowed no-shows? If so, how many are allowed? It can be helpful if there is a proforma letter which the therapist can send to clients who have failed to attend their sessions, setting out the client's position *vis-à-vis* the placement.

2 When and how fees are paid and collected. Is the therapist part of this system? What happens if fees are not paid? Note that the therapist might have personal feelings about this. If fees are administered electronically by the administration team it is less complicated.

3 How client referrals will be made: who does this and how does the therapist proceed with it? Crucial to this is clarity about how to make a first appointment with a client (more about this below).

4 The health and safety policies or procedures. These could include any significant safety issues relating to working in the building itself, e.g. the use of staircases, alarm buttons in therapy rooms, any other specific quirks of the building and site, and the fire alarm system. The handbook may also advise about the locking up procedures if the therapist will be the last one in the building in the evening, and any known challenges arising from the location of the agency.

5 How to administer outcome/assessment forms such as GAD 7 or PHQ-9 or CORE forms with a client.

Support and requirements for you as a member of the team

The trainee will have been advised whether they will receive in-house supervision at the placement. If the placement does not offer this, you will need to find out what they require concerning supervision – whether they consider supervision provided by your training organization (if you have one) or the amount of private supervision enough to cover the client load you will be holding for them. Be clear about the frequency of supervision or type of supervision you must adhere to, if the placement does not provide it.

Be clear about whether the placement provides professional malpractice insurance – usually called professional indemnity insurance. If this is not in place, the therapist will need to buy their own so as to have legal and financial cover should a complaint be made against them. Most placements do have a group insurance scheme, but always check.

Associated with the above is the question of who takes clinical responsibility for the work. This essentially means if something goes wrong during the work, who will be called to account for it – the placement, the training organization or the therapist? The most common position tends to be that the placement takes this responsibility, as they have offered the client the therapeutic contract and service. However, I have experience as a trainer of one agency in the past saying that the responsibility was shared with the training organization because we were training the therapist.

The agency may provide some specialist training before the start of clinical work, e.g. on bereavement or substance misuse, or they may offer additional training at another time. Are these voluntary or obligatory components of your contract with the agency? All of these, although useful, add to the time commitment.

Purely from the trainee perspective, check if the placement is willing to sign forms and/or write reports that your training organization requires. Most placements understand the need for these endorsements. However, bear in mind that placements are very busy and so try not to burden them with pieces of paper from the training organization. Get organized with paperwork so that it can be given as a batch to the appropriate person, usually the placement manager. Occasionally a trainee may have to pay for a supervision report or assessment written by a supervisor or manager.

Legal requirements and issues

As part of the offer, the placement will ask for a Disclosure and Barring Service (DBS) certificate. The purpose of supplying this is to help an employer – in this context the placement service – know whether they are recruiting suitable people to work in the placement. The DBS records convictions, cautions and reprimands that the person has received in the past.

The agency may require the trainee to have specific training on the Children Act 2004 or safeguarding, the Prevention of Terrorism Act 2005 and the Prevent duty guidance (2015). Trainees may be asked to complete an online course for the latter before or near the start of the placement. It may be that the training organization will already have covered these elements.

Becoming a member of a professional body

Before starting clinical work the therapist needs to become a trainee member of a professional organization such as the BACP or UKCP with an ethical framework or code of ethics. This is both to support the therapist as a member of a professional body, by providing advice and information on certain subjects, and to become part of a broader professional organization. Being a member of a professional body also protects the public by setting out standards for professional conduct and giving the public a recourse and protection against poor standards of practice. The psychotherapy and counselling professions are not regulated by law, so the professional bodies are regarded as the regulators of these professions. In joining the organization the trainee is agreeing to abide by the ethical policy of their professional body.

General points

The placement should make clear in their induction which elements of their administrative policies will be covered by the assessor who first meets the client, and which elements the therapist will need to discuss or reiterate with their client when meeting them for the first time. Clients can be very anxious when they come to an agency for an assessment, so may not have absorbed all the information about the contract details that the assessor has given. So it might be the case that the placement advises the therapist to go over some or all of the administrative procedures with the client.

Trying to grasp all of the above, and maybe more, can feel overwhelming to a new trainee. So be clear from the above about what has to be discussed with the client. Committing these formal administrative details to memory may preoccupy the trainee at the first meeting with the client. It is difficult to both keep in mind the administration of the agency and at the same time begin to build a therapeutic relationship with a client at the first meeting, but as trainees become more familiar with the policies of the agency, the need to follow procedure becomes more second nature, and the focus can shift to the psychological aspects of relationship building. This takes time to learn, but learning breeds confidence.

Assessment of clients

The prime difference between working in a placement as a trainee and working in private practice after qualifying is that in a placement setting a senior practitioner will have done an assessment of a potential client to determine their suitability for working with a trainee. This is for the safety and well-being of both the client and the therapist, so that there is a good enough match between them. The assessment is intended to ensure that the client will be working with someone with enough competency to deal with and work with their material, and that the therapist has a client with a history and issues deemed suitable for the therapist's level of competency and experience. With psychological services under increasing pressure to take more complex cases, making this therapeutic fit is challenging; it is part of the ethical consideration and practice within a placement to make as appropriate a match as possible.

The quality of the assessment is crucial. However, in practice assessments vary – some are done in person with the prospective client coming into the building, whilst others are done over the phone or, since Covid-19, online. In best practice, by talking to the prospective client the assessor records a substantial client history to determine how complex their issues are and their suitability to be taken on for counselling or psychotherapy. The assessor considers in particular if the potential client is suitable for time-limited work – 6 or 12 sessions – or whether longer or open-ended work is more appropriate for them. If the placement does not make an assessment, it is inadvisable for a new trainee with no experience to take this placement. Some training organizations will not allow the trainee to take up a placement in these circumstances, for the safety of the service user and to protect the trainee from an unsuitable referral.

A caveat: in a few placements that do not provide an assessment process the placement will ask the trainee to compile a history, using a set format of questions (on an intake form) which the trainee uses to record the client information. Then the trainee meets their supervisor to discuss whether the client is suitable for what the placement offers and if the client is suitable for the trainee. It is important that *no* promise of therapeutic work is made to the client before the discussion with the supervisor has taken place. Additionally, the trainee needs to be clear whether they want to follow this intake procedure, especially if this is their first clinical placement, and that will need to be agreed by the training organization.

I strongly feel that new trainees should not be asked to take a client history/ gather initial information. Even with a structure like an intake form this is a complex task, and is best left for a senior member of staff who can record the history and assess the client whilst building a rapport with them.

Outcome measures

Some placements use outcome measures as part of their assessment for potential clients. Without going into the details of these measures, it is important that the trainee has some knowledge of the higher scores which indicate that a client is not suitable for work with a new trainee. For CORE OM, scores of 20–25 mean moderate to severe distress, and over 25 severe distress. For Patient Health Questionnaire-9 (PHQ-9), scores of 15–19 indicate moderately severe and 20–27 severe distress. For GAD-7: Anxiety Severity, 10–14 indicates moderate anxiety and 15–21 severe anxiety.

Referral of a client to a therapist within an agency

The assessor then gives the therapist some information about the client. They may send an electronic copy of the assessment report or leave it in the office, or arrange to have a conversation with the therapist over the phone or online. The therapist then needs to decide if they want to take on this client. On rare occasions a trainee therapist declines the referral of a client after serious consideration with their supervisor or sometimes their tutor. It is a courageous and ethical response to be able to say 'No, this client is not right for me at this point.' This is not easy to do, especially if this is the first referral. The trainee needs to be able to reflect on and articulate why they have made this decision. On the whole, placements are willing to accept the trainee's decision providing they understand the reason for it and providing the trainee does not refuse every client! It is a common reaction on receiving information about the first client that it all seems impossible and too much. However, the training organization will have affirmed that they think you are ready to start clinical work, and the fact that the agency has offered you a placement is an indication that they have faith in you to begin working with their service users.

Making first contact with the client

After the client has been assessed, the usual first contact with the client is made by the trainee over the phone. This is important because you hear each other's voices and a personal contact is made. In addition, the start of a working alliance – i.e. an arrangement for the first meeting – is agreed between the two of you.

To keep this discussion focused and clear, prepare before phoning by making sure the call is made from a quiet and private space. Be clear about what to say to the client about arrangements for starting the work together.

Start by confirming that you are the therapist from the placement. Ask the client if it is a good time to speak: if not, when might be suitable? Note: it has to be suitable for the therapist as well, so offer some alternative times. Then make the offer of the date and time of the first session to the client, all the while noticing any hesitation or confusion in them. Check with the client that they have understood the details of the appointment. If the client was initially assessed over the phone or online it is useful to check if the client is clear about the address, how they gain entry to the building and where they can wait if they are early.

If the client tries to tell details of their story at this point, quietly but firmly stop them going further, guiding them to wait until you meet in person.

If online work is offered, be clear about the procedure for making contact. First, the therapist gives the online contact details to the client, or explains how the contact details will be sent to them, e.g. by email link, having established that this mode of communication is suitable and accessible for the client. Also agree a backup plan in case of online technological difficulties. This usually means agreeing to make contact by phone or mobile, and who will call the other. In most cases the therapist attempts to call the client should these difficulties occur.

Trainee voice – first contact

'It may be easier for some clients to have the first contact by email rather than to have a phone call out of the blue.'

Therapist preparation before the first meeting with the client

Getting to the stage of meeting a first client is the fruition of what it's all about. So it is a very significant moment for the trainee. The approaching first appointment with a client is full of psychological meaning, excitement and anxiety – all in varying degrees, and probably constantly changing. Professional and psychological preparation beforehand helps.

Professional practice includes readiness to start the session at the appointed time by being early (last-minute rushes increase anxiety), having the room prepared (if there is access to it beforehand), having an online room prepared – tidy and neutral – having any forms ready to give to the client, and being clear about the procedure concerning fees and money.

Personal preparation about what to wear and feeling comfortable in what you are wearing can be reassuring for the new trainee. Leave any designer clothes and jewellery at home. The attention needs to be on the client, not the therapist's appearance.

Trainee voices – preparing for a first client

'I found the prospect of my first client daunting – but the support I have had through my training organization and agency supervision has really helped me to find my feet.'

'It was extremely helpful to me to talk it over in supervision, focusing on the basics and active listening instead of trying to shine with insight and be smart. Meditation or grounding before the session was also helpful. Also, it is a given that most if not all trainees will be nervous before a first client, so just accept it. Plus, as soon as the trainee begins to really listen to the client, the anxiety will go because she won't be focused on herself any more.'

And here is a checklist before starting.

Join or organize:

- *professional body – get student membership*
- *insurance – do I need to get my own instead of/on top of agency indemnity?*
- *Zoom – get your own account and practise setting up appointments with a classmate*
- *workspace for remote work – decide on a neutral home workspace*
- *social media profile – Google yourself and where necessary anonymize/ protect social media accounts so clients won't find you*
- *ICO.*

Refamiliarize myself with:

- *ethical framework or code of ethics – reread*
- *risk plan – make sure I know in advance what to do if a client presents as a risk during a session*
- *contracting – prepare a checklist of points to cover during contracting.*

Training requirements:

- *forms – complete all forms between training organization and placement and return to tutors.*

Meeting the client in person or online

The first hurdle is the moment of meeting. In most placements the therapist meets the client in a waiting area or at the front door. If the therapist is meeting the client for the first time in a space that is also occupied by other clients, they maintain confidentiality by asking, 'Who is waiting for X?' (saying your name). Or do a quick assessment of who is in the waiting room, make an educated guess and approach the person you think fits the description of your client. Then quietly ask them 'are you Y?' – using their first name only. Clients in an anxious state may have forgotten the therapist's name, so be prepared to go for different angles of approach. Overall, discretion is the key here.

The second challenge is the walk to the therapy room, which can feel awkward. It's best not to engage with the client on this journey. Clients who are anxious may try to engage the therapist in some kind of talk or ask questions. It may be their way of trying to get to know their therapist before sitting down in the therapy room. All of these comments and questions are best left to be part of the therapy, which starts when the door shuts!

Arriving at the therapy room itself and entering the room brings up the question of who leads the way and why. There are no hard rules about this, and it is often a personal choice of the therapist whether to lead the way or indicate to the client to go ahead. This brings up the next issue: how does the therapist decide on the seating arrangements, or can the client choose where to sit? It is clearer if the therapist walks into the room first and indicates to the client where to sit. This option could be experienced as organized and professional, but it could also be experienced by the client as part of the power dynamics and control in the relationship.

Meeting online: if this is the first time you see the client, tactfully check they are who you expect them to be. Putting the waiting room security button on (in Zoom accounts) will show the name of the person in the waiting room. This can help to avoid mistakes by admitting the wrong person. Additionally, if using the same Meeting ID and passcode for every client rather than issuing individual invitations, be careful that another client hasn't inadvertently joined the online room at the wrong time. There are pros and cons to keeping the same online details with every client and for issuing new invitations for every meeting. The placement may suggest how best to do this.

Transition from assessor to therapist

Having invited the client into the therapy room and invited them to sit down, the therapist needs to start to build a rapport with them.

In an online setting, check with them if they are safe and comfortable in their surroundings and that the audio is working. It is good to reiterate the emergency plan for failure of technology at the start of the session. Some basic containment around the time limit of the session is a useful boundary to establish early in this first meeting with the client.

Prior information from the assessment

How to talk with a client about their experience of meeting the assessor, and their move to a therapist, often feels difficult. The crux of the matter seems to be: what do I say I know about you, the client, that has come from the assessor?

At the same time the client may be wondering what you know about them. If the therapist has read the assessment notes or has had a conversation with the assessor, they will know information about the client. Keeping this fact a secret is not being congruent towards the client.

It is worth considering how the therapist views the assessment notes or information they have been given before meeting the client. In general the assessment is a useful initial body of information for the new trainee to hold lightly in mind. Sometimes a client has told the assessor a lot of information which may not re-emerge in the therapy for some time. It's a bit like telling your life story to a stranger on a train that you will never meet again. Whatever was revealed in the assessment is not the full story of the client's experience and it is not the working through of the story and the deep emotional processes imbued in it, which will happen over time in the therapeutic work.

Talking about the move from assessor to therapist

The transfer from the assessor to the therapist is an essential foundation stone for the therapeutic relationship. Begin by acknowledging that the client has met and spoken with the assessor, in person or remotely. Clients may have had a very good experience of meeting the assessor and will have been relieved to have had their story heard. Consequently some clients do not quite take in the fact that the assessor will not be their therapist.

During this discussion it is critical to notice whether the client seems to be reacting to the 'loss' of the assessor. If a strong rapport was built during the assessment session the client might find the transition to the new therapist difficult and destabilizing. While acknowledging the loss of the assessor, it is a good moment to reiterate that a new and ongoing therapeutic relationship with you is being offered. Making this professional transfer of relationship explicit is important. It is vital to check that the client has grasped and accepted the situation, and if not, to understand what their difficultly or concern is about in terms of making a new relationship.

What does the therapist need to know in more detail?

The therapist, having made explicit that they have some prior information about the client, should consider whether this is enough to say in this meeting. As a rule of thumb, there is no need to go into specific detail about what is known from the assessment. However, it is essential to check that the issue that the client came with in the first place is still what the client wants to work on, especially if there has been a long waiting period for the client before starting in therapy.

Before meeting the client the therapist may be left with questions from the assessment information which still seem pressing. It would be very useful if they could have supervision before meeting the client to have an opportunity to discuss the client's background and what it might be useful to know more about.

Determining whether it is the therapist's anxiety about the need to know something, or if a piece of information is crucial, shows the necessity for further reflection. It is a clinical decision in itself in deciding what is important to know at a particular time. If the therapist finds not knowing unbearable, confusing or worrying, this needs acknowledging and examining in the therapist's own personal development space. Often new trainees want to know too much too soon, as it can create anxiety within themselves to sit with the unknown and the unclear. Having information can give a sense of feeling in control or being competent, when the underlying feelings may be of incompetence and of being out of control.

The desire to clarify some detail is not a licence to bombard the client with questions in this first meeting. If there is a detail of fact that is not clear, the therapist can say that they wish to check or clarify a piece of information – e.g. if the assessment notes record 'partner died' it may be relevant to enquire if this has been a recent bereavement. However, resist the temptation to ask too much. It can leave the new and anxious client feeling put on the spot or intruded upon. It may be best to hold onto the question for now and bring it back nearer the end of the session, when the relationship has started to form. Often if the therapist waits and listens well, the client will supply the information. This first transition session includes one of the many clinical judgements that centre around 'when' and 'how' the therapist could say or ask something.

Making the contract with the client

It is essential to discuss and clarify the therapeutic contract with the client so that it forms a basic building block for the therapeutic relationship.

Clients seek help because they know something is not working in their life or because someone else, a partner or a colleague, has a sense that the person is in difficulty. In the best interests of the working alliance (Bordin, 1979), both therapeutic partners need to become clearer about what the client wants from the work and to clarify whether this is feasible within the boundaries of what is being offered by the placement. Clients who have had no experience of a therapeutic intervention may erroneously think that coming to a therapist will somehow magically make them better. For the therapy to work, the client needs to engage and become a participant in the work. Making a contract with the client will help them to engage in and take some responsibility for the therapeutic work.

The contract with the client has essentially two elements to it, the first being what I call the procedural or business contract, which may have been already discussed and agreed between the assessor and client. (Be clear about what the assessor has said about this and what paperwork the assessor has shown the client.) On the assumption that the assessor has made a business contract, the therapist still needs to briefly restate the contents of this, specifically pertaining to what has been offered, i.e. the number of sessions, the time of sessions, the placement's cancellation policy and fees, and the limits of confidentiality.

Clients, especially if they have never experienced any psychological intervention, may not have digested what was discussed in the assessment meeting.
Recapping the contract gives another chance to solidify understanding of what
is being offered by the placement and what is required of the client. This is part
of the fundamental containment for the therapeutic work and should not be
neglected or minimized. It sets the framework and lays the foundations for the
working alliance.

Intrinsic to creating a safe frame for the therapeutic journey is how the limits of confidentiality are explained to the client in this first meeting. The basic
points centre on stating that the work is confidential but there are some circumstances under which confidentiality might be broken. Be clear with the client
that confidentiality may be broken if there is a situation or circumstances
where there may be harm to the client or to someone else. The therapist can
expand on this by stating that they will endeavour to speak with the client
about the situation before breaking confidentiality. Additionally state that if
the client makes a disclosure about money laundering or an act of terrorism,
then confidentiality will be broken. Clarity in describing these fundamental ethical and legal boundaries is crucial. The therapist needs to know what their
placement's position is, especially if they are working in statutory services or
with vulnerable client groups.

Watch for a client's hesitation or concern about these limits of confidentiality and find a way to bring this into an open discussion so that the client can
express their concerns or fears. The client needs to be clear about what the
therapist may have to disclose about them. Being clear increases trust and
helps the client to feel safe enough to begin telling their story.

The second element is the making of the therapeutic contract. Listening to
the client's narrative and reasons for what has led them to seek therapy, and
why now – i.e. the immediate trigger – starts the process. Be mindful that there
may have been a long wait between the time of the assessment and the client
arriving at the first session. It is then useful to ask if the client's circumstances
or reasons for seeking therapy have changed.

Having heard their ostensible reasons for coming to therapy, there needs to
be further discussion and negotiation about what the client wants from the
therapy. Often this enquiry gets a vague response, but it is worth taking some
time to help the client become clearer in their own mind about what they want
from the sessions. The client may not be aware of the difference between what
they think they want from therapy and what they may really need, especially if
the client is in a highly charged or stressed state when they reach the session.
Be mindful that what brings the client through the door may not be what the
deeper issue is about. Nevertheless, inviting the client to articulate what they
want can foster a sense that the client is an agent in this process, not a passive
recipient, thereby strengthening the therapeutic alliance. In addition, discussing the client's fantasies about what will or could happen in the work, and the
clarifying of unrealistic expectations, can assist in setting out what the respective roles of the two participants entail. Taking the time to have this conversation can pay dividends in the work, which enhances the sense that there are

two people in the room working together for the client's benefit. Without this negotiated, you-and-I dialogue, the client will be left feeling something is being done to them by the therapist. It may adversely create a sense that the therapist knows everything and does everything in the work, and that the client only needs to show up in order to be healed. If this erroneous thinking persists the therapy will soon, if not immediately stall because no solid foundations for a working alliance have been laid.

Creating a strong therapeutic alliance is what I see as the CART which carries the work forward. Its essential ingredients are:

- the Collaboration between the two participants
- the explicit Aims of the therapeutic work
- the respective Responsibilities of the two participants
- and the bedrock of Trust for the therapy, which is built over time between the two participants but starts at the first meeting.

All through this first meeting the therapist needs to be continually aware of what is happening in the room in order to see how the client is responding and/or reacting, what is happening between themselves and the client, and noticing their own initial responses to the client. This is a tall order for new therapists, but the capacity to observe these dynamics comes with practice.

For the first session(s) with your first client(s), getting through it is enough. Believe that you will be able to build and develop the therapeutic relationship as you begin to feel more comfortable in the therapist's chair.

Possible dynamics in the first meeting

It is common in this first meeting to notice signs of anxiety and ambivalence in a client. At one level this is a completely natural reaction for a client to have, especially for a client who has never been to therapy before. It usually stems from doubt and anxiety about engaging in therapy, shown in comments such as, 'I don't know why I have come' and 'I think I will be wasting your time.' These throwaway comments are not to be ignored. Directly but sensitively asking the client what is their fear about embarking on therapy can prove to be useful. The question could illuminate deeper fears about trust. Can I trust the therapist? Can I trust myself to explore? Can I trust going into the unknown? This exploration may give an indication of fears about who holds power in the relationship. The client may be consciously or unconsciously thinking about the therapist – will you have power to control me, manipulate me or judge me? Having these thoughts possibly indicates that the client is being affected by other experiences of seeking help. Whilst it may not be appropriate at this moment to start to open up these unconscious dynamics, it is often a relief for the client to have shared their deep fear about what might happen and to have an opportunity to discuss it with the therapist. Beginning to allow a client to express their hidden fears about being in therapy ironically can increase the level of trust between the participants and in the process.

If the client has openly said they have been 'sent' to therapy it is crucial to establish some motivation from the client about embarking on the work, otherwise there will be no collaboration and the client will not take responsibility for the work. It is likely that the client will be either resentful or suspicious about being in the room with a stranger when it was not their plan! Delicate discussion to endeavour to open up what the client is thinking and feeling about being sent to therapy can help the client feel heard. This is particularly important if the client has a history of multiple professional interventions and now has this new compulsory 'treatment' foisted upon them. A deep reticence about professional help or their attitude to the person who 'sent' them will only threaten the potential working alliance of this new therapy. Don't try to prove to them that therapy is useful for them; instead, give them the experience of someone listening to them in a respectful way in order to understand them. Ultimately the client will decide, consciously or unconsciously, whether they want to continue and engage with their own journey.

Trainee voice – the therapeutic contract

In class discussion the following points were made about some of the difficulties making a therapeutic contract:

- *Client not being clear about their goals*
- *Client expecting too much*
- *Client has pre-existing beliefs and biases about counsellors*
- *Client not knowing how therapy works – expecting advice or CBT*
- *Trust not yet established in the relationship*
- *Worry that the counsellor can't take the client's issues*
- *Probation, not voluntarily in therapy*
- *Waiting time from assessment – situation may have changed*

Trainee voice – what helps to overcome these issues

- *Work together on thinking about goal(s), ask if anything has changed since assessment or refer to assessment notes*
- *Reflect goals back to client*
- *Be realistic about what's achievable*
- *Ask them what their preconceptions are*
- *Ask about previous experiences of therapy*
- *Explain how we work*
- *Be honest about trust taking time*
- *Go at client's pace*
- *Show openness and understanding to the client*

Building trust

Making contact with the client at the initial meeting is a critical element in building trust in the therapeutic relationship; it is also the beginning of building rapport with the client. If there is one main component in the earliest sessions with the client which builds the foundations for trust and safety in the work, it is the therapist's capacity to really listen to the client's story.

In new trainees the pressure to get it right – whatever they think 'right' is: say something clever to prove they are competent, make a brilliant interpretation, illuminate the relational dynamics or say or do something that will save the client – is somewhere in the mix, either consciously or unconsciously. Becoming aware of these anxieties or pressures to do well or succeed is important. To counteract these tendencies, the new therapist needs to keep firmly in their mind that therapeutic intervention at its most basic and most refined levels is the art of listening and responding appropriately.

Self-reflection

- *What pressure might you put on yourself when you are starting out?*
- *Consider where this pressure may come from in your own history.*

Listening

New therapists often underestimate the importance of listening well to the client. It is worth keeping in mind that many traumas in the client's life may have come from experiences of not being heard and the subsequent wounds that are created out of those missed experiences. The client will have a sense of whether the therapist is really listening to them or not. If the therapist does not listen well, the capacity to understand the client and help them understand themselves will be diminished.

Listening to the client is a complex process. It involves:

- The ability to track the client's story whilst noticing how and when the client's narrative or part of the narrative becomes confused, vague, chaotic or disjointed.
- Noticing the dynamics of how the client is presenting their story in the room verbally and non-verbally. In fact, most of the important information about the client's internal world is conveyed through the client's voice and manner of speech, the rhythm of the speech, the breaks in the flow and in the quality of their silences; changes in the client's body movements may also be significant.
- Noticing what the client is saying and what the client is not saying about any given experience.
- Noticing how the client is looking at the therapist – in the eye, or turning away, or looking down. These are not just behavioural responses, but clues to the client's inner state in that moment in relation to the therapist and about themselves.
- The capacity of the therapist to listen with curiosity and an open thinking mind to their client's story.
- The patience of the therapist to be able to wait for the story to unfold.

The quality and depth of listening that happens in the room comes from the quality of presence emanating from the therapist. (In observed skills practice sessions a peer observer or tutor can readily see or sense this quality of presence. It is very obvious when it's not there.) So for the new trainee, settling down into a calm and prepared, focused state, having put aside their own personal concerns for the time being, facilitates the emergence of an attentive listener. All of these attributes assist the therapist in tuning more and more finely into the experience of their client.

Responding

Listening engenders a response in the therapist, whether or not the therapist says something explicitly to the client. In building the initial trust stage of the work with the client (or in later stages of the work if there has been a rupture), the client needs to have it confirmed that the therapist has heard them.

Using the core reflective skills as identified by Culley (1991) – restating, summarizing and paraphrasing – demonstrates that at the narrative level the therapist has heard what the client has said. These are often elements of the basic skill set which have been taught during the preclinical year of training. They are absolutely essential in training the ear of the therapist to shift from conversational mode into a more disciplined therapeutic way of responding.

In addition to this, the client needs to feel *emotionally heard*; thus the therapist's ability to attune (Stern 1985) and empathize (Rogers 1957) with them is crucial. For the therapist to understand and *show they understand* the emotion and emotional energy behind the client's words is like putting in the cement that holds the foundations in place. These attuned and empathic responses are conveyed through the therapist's non-verbal communication, as much as by the therapist's actual words.

In short, in the early sessions, the therapist demonstrates that they are listening to and can respond empathically to their client. This will go a long way in building the foundations for the therapeutic alliance with a client. New trainees try to do too much too soon – partly because they are enthusiastic about new skills and ideas they are learning, and partly because of internal and sometimes external pressure to demonstrate the use of skills and theoretical ideas in practice. If in doubt, wait longer. I have told students who intervene too quickly to count to five in their head before making an intervention. It buys the trainee time to think before speaking. It also allows the client to think further about what they have said and what they might say next. See more on this in Chapter 9, Working with feelings.

The first review

There is usually a review of the work with a client after the first four to six sessions. Doing this first review may feel daunting to the new trainee, who may feel that the review is mainly a scorecard on their work. It's best to see the review as an opportunity for the client to voice their experience of being in therapy. The client may allude to what the therapist is doing well in the work and indicate what they still need.

Depending on the strength of the therapist's internal critic, any feedback could be taken as a help in developing the work with the client, or it could be viewed as a discouraging or critical remark about the therapist. Sometimes when the client says 'this is not helping' it is predominantly a statement about the client's processes – how they are engaging or not with the work. If, however, the therapist is very self-critical it may be taken primarily as a comment on their competency. As the therapist gains more experience, these review sessions become more useful as a therapeutic barometer which records the psychological energy of the therapeutic alliance and assists in showing the way forward for the work rather than as a comment about the therapist.

If the placement is using formal measures (e.g. GAD 7, PHQ-9 or CORE OM), if these have not been discussed with the client on a regular basis the review session is an opportunity to talk about how the client feels about doing them and if there are any difficulties around filling them in. One trainee began to realize that a client was struggling with reading the forms. She very discreetly suggested that she read the questions to the client and filled in the client's answers on the forms. Some clients may simply be averse to filling in forms. Although this form filling is administrative, there is also the opportunity for more therapeutic discussions around the significance of the scoring or parts of the scoring on the forms, especially if scores increase. Therapist and client can notice changes in the scoring and consider the meaning and importance of these changes, which can be fruitful.

Making connections and asking for support

In a supportive placement these first few weeks are important for laying the foundations for the new therapist's confidence. They need to feel and acknowledge that they have survived the first session, have maintained the initial work up to the point of review, have started to engage with peers and a supervisor, and begun learning in a clinical setting. All of this will help the therapist to feel part of the organization.

It is also important for the well-being of the therapist to find support from someone in the placement when feeling unsure or challenged by something that has happened. It may be that supervision in the placement is the place to take this concern; otherwise seek out the coordinator or manager. If you know that a concern is about an old familiar feeling or thought pattern, for example 'I'm not good enough', then this is most fruitfully explored in personal therapy. Work with our clients can awaken the demons within us either briefly or over a longer period.

Complaints

If a client makes a complaint against the therapist it is the placement's duty to investigate the nature of the complaint, by talking with the client in the first instance and then hearing the therapist's account and the supervisor's view on the competency and ethical stance of the therapist. Usually the complaint is resolved through this process. If the placement upholds the client's complaint the placement will need to contact the training organization to pass on the outcome of the investigation. Both the placement and the training organization will make a decision about the therapist's fitness to practise.

Overall

The early sessions can feel very demanding for the new trainee. See each session as a step to learning. Learning includes making slip-ups and mistakes, which are keenly felt when new in practice. The positive aspect in all of this is the lessons learned as a result. Professionally, as confidence grows, there will be an increased sense of self as a therapist. This all starts through the opportunity to work in a clinical placement, but it continues throughout the therapist's career. Being in supervision is a crucial part of this.

3   Tests of boundaries

One trainee I supervised had a client who over a period of time failed to pay their fee on the day of the session (in the days when cash reigned in placements!). This then progressed to paying only part of the fee in the session and eventually to failing to pay anything at all. The trainee was very diligent about recording what the client paid and was also able to discuss with the client if they had financial difficulties in paying, which the client denied. In this difficult situation supervision was a place to consider the meaning of what was happening. The trainee was able to be curious and reflective about the deeper meaning of these tests of boundaries and bring it into the relationship with their client for discussion and exploration. They also had to consider why they had let the matter slip without bringing it for discussion in supervision or with the placement coordinator.

When boundaries are broken by the client it can have repercussions on the therapist – often leaving them not knowing what to do, feeling confused or incompetent or out of control in the situation. These can cause anxiety in the therapist. All of these feelings can inhibit the therapist from challenging the client appropriately. Tests of boundaries are in many cases challenges to the therapeutic contract and beyond this the therapeutic relationship itself.

When therapists break boundaries there are implications for their professional and ethical practice.

Tests to commitment

The first session. The practical arrangement regarding the time of a session is the first test of a boundary and a reflection of some deeper process within the client. Usually the therapist or the administrator has confirmed the time of the first meeting between therapist and client. It is preferable for the therapist to contact the client to make this appointment as it confirms the start of their therapeutic relationship, but this is not always what happens. Clients who want to change the arrangement or fail to keep the first appointment are very likely to be anxious about starting their therapy, even though they have come into the placement for the initial assessment or had an assessment online. Depending on the reason the client gives, a new appointment may be offered. If a client again fails to attend the first appointment it is a sign that they are not ready or too anxious to begin therapy at this time. The placement may not offer them a new appointment.

Being late. The second indication of underlying emotions and processes is lateness in attending sessions. Whilst there is a real life outside the therapy room which exists in terms of transport and people getting the flu, or emergency situations, persistent lateness or lateness occurring after a difficult or challenging session or a holiday break needs to be discussed with the client. The therapist needs to raise this issue with their client. This can be done by stating the fact that you are aware of the client arriving late for their session and then inviting the client to think about what being late might mean for them. If the therapist thinks the client has been late because the previous session or sessions have been challenging or disturbing for the client, they need to empathically convey an understanding of the client's possible fears about what might happen in a full-length session.

Clients sometimes come online late because of losing sign-in details or having trouble signing in online. Sometimes computers don't work or mobiles have run out of charge. There are real technology difficulties and some people are more confident using technology than others, but it is also worth pondering if these difficulties have other meanings, especially if they persist over time.

If being late for a session is also part of an erratic attendance pattern to sessions, there is an ambivalence in the client about being in therapy. Has the client given you any hints about what their ambivalence is about? Is there a reluctance about being in therapy? For example, they might have been sent to therapy by their GP, as a result of their partner's influence or insistence, or as part of a probation order. This reluctance or ambivalence to come to sessions needs to be discussed, or the work will not get off the ground.

Changing session time. A caveat to the above is the client wanting to change the time or day of the session. The therapist has to determine with the client what are the practical implications of this request. In some placements there is very little flexibility for change, either because of the therapist's availability or availability of the room. If a client is requesting such a big change it often means that the client is put back into the referral system to start again with a new therapist. The therapist needs to consider if this is a comment on the therapeutic relationship or something very practical in the client's life.

Cancellations. A bane for therapists is the client who frequently cancels a session, and especially if the client makes last-minute cancellations. Trainees have put aside precious time to make their commitment to the placement, maybe seeing three people in quick succession. These cancellations, or at worst 'no shows', can feel crushing, especially if the therapist is tired and has made a tremendous effort to fulfil their commitment. Therapeutically there is some meaning in this cancellation in terms of the client's experience. Anxiety is often the culprit. However, it can feel very disrespectful to the therapist, especially if this is a recurring event. It is also disrespectful to the placement, as on paper the therapist is still holding this client on their books instead of being available to take on new clients. It's not always easy for new trainees to see the disrespect as opposed to the anxiety in these actions. In effect, these actions mean the therapist, the placement and clients on the waiting lists for the service are all affected.

Contact outside session time. Linked to the above, there is the practical issue of how contact is made outside session time. In some placements messages from clients only go through the reception staff so that the therapist's contact details are kept private. In principle this is a good idea, but practically there can be difficulties in messages getting through to the therapist in good time. Letting your client have a mobile contact number gets round the problem of messages not being passed on. I have heard of one or two placements that give their therapists separate mobile phones for the work or advise therapists to get a pay-as-you-go mobile that is only used for placement work. The disadvantage of using a single mobile for both professional and personal use is that a message could be sent inadvertently to a client instead of a friend, and vice versa. But having a mobile does facilitate direct contact between therapist and client without the need for messages to be passed through a third party. Using a mobile necessitates registering with the Information Commissioner's Office (ICO) as the therapist is keeping confidential data – a client's phone number – on an electronic device.

Two issues to be mindful of when speaking to a client on a mobile are: first, is it convenient and confidential to speak to them at that time? Secondly, when speaking to a client by phone other than to rearrange a session, keep these conversations short and non-therapeutic. This is also the case with text messages or emails from a client, unless you are trained in offering asynchronous therapy. These exchanges are not for therapeutic input unless there is an emergency situation that the therapist has to assess and respond to immediately.

Breaking the contract of the agency

Placements that have clearly stated policies about the use of substances before attending therapy (e.g. no drugs or alcohol for 24 hours before a session) need to be backed up by the therapist. If the therapist suspects a client is breaking this agreement they need to be able to address it directly with the client as soon as possible. If this behaviour persists, then discuss a way forward with the clinical manager in the placement. It will be of no help to allow the client to break the specific 'rule', and it will make the therapist complicit with the client against the placement. If in your heart you don't believe in the agency policy, it is a sign of your integrity to relinquish this placement. There needs to be a congruence between your attitude and beliefs and those held by the agency.

Trainee voice – bringing baby to the session

'A client brought her 14-month-old baby to a session when the childcare was late. This was an incredibly challenging moment as it required an immediate

response. Although she had asked early on if this would be ok and we had discussed that this wouldn't be possible, she still came so it felt like a test of boundaries. I brought them into the counselling room for privacy and spent a few minutes talking about the session not being possible for health and safety reasons, acknowledging that she might really like the session to go ahead. It felt very uncomfortable to have to cancel the session and I anticipated that a rupture would need to be repaired. I felt heartless and it felt difficult not being able to support her in that moment, but I knew it wasn't safe and we wouldn't be able to work together with the baby present. When she returned the following week we discussed this impact on the baby, on her, and how we might both hold back in order to protect the baby. We subsequently worked with her irritation at me for sending them away, which enabled my client to process her anger and recognize how difficult it was for her to be honest about her feelings.'

Tests of boundaries online

This mainly centres on two things. First, the client needs to speak from an appropriate private and safe place. It can be difficult for clients to keep their space private and distraction-free if they are at home. Some placements clearly state that they will not allow clients to phone their therapists whilst sitting in a car. The other issue is about the client being appropriately dressed.

Trainee voice – testing boundaries

'Due to Covid I did a lot of client work remotely – this seemed to give clients many opportunities to test the boundaries. I've experienced clients joining sessions whilst driving, making their lunch, in a hospital waiting room, and still in bed. If the situation was unethical, unsafe, or breached confidentiality, I gently ended the session, explaining why, and agreed to meet again next time.'

The essence of working with these tests of boundaries can be summed up as:

'I found addressing these breaches as closely as possible to when they occur with clients not only helped to keep sessions contained but also when explored offered an opportunity to learn more about my clients' internal frame of reference.'

Other boundary tests

There are other ways in which a client can test or break boundaries in the therapeutic setting.

End-of-session boundary issues

A common boundary issue at the end of a session is if the client does not heed or act on the therapist's words for closing the session. Instead, the client continues to talk, and may take a long time to put their coat on, collect their bag and physically move out of the room. New therapists find this difficult to manage and often take these issues to supervision. The therapist needs to find ways and interventions to encourage the client to leave the room, which range from subtle cues to direct interventions, and even reviewing the therapeutic contract with the client. The therapist may have to stand up before the client stands, move to the door of the room and indicate that they are about to open the door. If these cues don't work, the therapist will need to be more direct with the client by reminding them that the session is over. Again if this persists over the course of the work the difficulty in leaving needs to be talked over with the client at the beginning of a session. Online it is technically easier as the therapist can end the session by ending the meeting. However, the therapist would need to examine with the client why they find it difficult to ready themselves for the end of the session. All of this is full of meaning – consciously or not!

There is also what is known as the 'doorknob comment' delivered at the door of the therapy room (usually) or the front door, which means the therapist has no space or time to respond appropriately. An example could be 'I don't know how I will get through the week.' A doorknob comment can feel like a hit-and-run experience. It can leave the therapist stunned and disempowered, or anxious if the client hints at destructive behaviour. Rarely are they comments full of joy which the client forgot to make in the therapy room. Essentially they close down the therapist at that point and the most they can say is that this can be discussed next time. However, the doorknob comment may well be significant and should be kept in mind. It is interesting to notice if the client brings it back in some form in the next or following sessions. It may be up to the therapist to reintroduce the comment at the beginning of the next session for exploration, both in what it meant to the client at the time and its meaning within the therapeutic relationship.

For example, 'You said at the front door that you were not sure how you would get through the week. I wonder why you were not able to say this to me earlier in the session?' Therapists take different views on this according to their therapeutic modality. Taking this to supervision before the next session with the client is the best course of action. As a rule of thumb I would be inclined to discuss the comment with the client if there were undertones of suicidal thoughts or hints of dissatisfaction about the therapy.

Money issues

Another indication of something happening either in the relationship or within the client is their attitude and behaviour around money. In most instances the fee for the session is usually agreed during the meeting with the assessor. However, some placements leave it up for negotiation between the therapist and the client as it is regarded as part of the therapeutic contract. The client's attitude towards paying for the service can denote many different things.

Difficulties arise when a client does not pay the agreed fee. Money and its meaning, through the payment or non-payment of fees, is part of the exchange between the therapeutic partners. The therapist needs to discuss the implications of 'money' issues with their client. It is the therapist who has to deal with this issue, so the therapist also has to reflect on their own attitude to money, paying fees and asking people in distress to pay for a service, in this context the therapist's help.

Self-reflection

- *How do you feel about asking clients to pay for the service?*
- *How do you think you would respond to clients who claim they have no money?*
- *What would be the most challenging thing you would have to face with regard to money issues in a placement?*

Some clients have a sense of entitlement to a free service. It is in the best interests of clarity if the placement's website and literature clearly state the charity or voluntary status of the placement and that donations or fees are requested or required from the users of the service. The therapist can then reiterate that there was an initial agreement about the fee and enquire if there are difficulties that have arisen around paying it. Most agencies do have a discretionary attitude towards clients who are in financial difficulties – for example, through loss of benefits or employment difficulties – and will therefore be willing to renegotiate the fee. The therapist must be clear about the procedure for doing this, i.e. whether they can renegotiate the fee with the client or if this has to be referred back to the assessor or manager of the service.

Paying the fee is also the mark of the investment a client makes in themselves in the therapy. It puts a value on the work and is a sign of willingness to participate in it. If the service is free it can engender a 'take it or leave it' attitude in some clients, which does not help to cement the working partnership of the therapy.

Making a monetary contribution is also a sign of gratitude for the service. In a few cases this can have more complicated emotional and hidden implications. A client on a low fee may be so grateful that they don't tell the therapist what's really wrong with them – so keeping elements of themselves and their behaviour out of the room in order to present themselves as worthy enough to use the service. Or the client may feel so grateful that they don't tell the therapist what they don't find helpful about how the therapist works. This is an unfortunate missed opportunity which places the onus on the therapist to consider what is not being said about the work.

Gifts

I think the days are gone when a therapist would not accept a small gift from a client at the end of the work. I believe most therapists would hold the view that it would be quite impolite – even hostile – to insist on declining the gift at the end of the work.

As trainees are working in a placement rather than private practice, many clients know that their therapist is a volunteer and therefore may wish to show some appreciation for the work by bringing a gift on the last session. The placement may have a policy about gifts. One placement I have heard about suggests that gifts are shared between the volunteers – that's easy if it's chocolate or some other consumable. Others are OK with small gifts being offered to the therapist. In the above circumstances there is rarely a problem. What does become problematic is a client who frequently brings a gift or hints that one is coming soon, or brings a gift that is inappropriate because it is too lavish or too personal. It is a moot point about what is too personal. Regarding the latter, some clients have given small pieces of jewellery to their therapist at the end of the work which, although personal and very thoughtful, still seems to be within the bounds of what is appropriate. The crucial point is what it says about the relationship and its termination. Essentially, does it feel right and proper? If there is no explicit policy and you feel unhappy or disquieted about the gift, bring it to supervision for discussion.

A supervisee of mine was in a challenging relationship with a client. This particular client liked making marmalade and brought the therapist a jar of their own marmalade as a Christmas gift. We spent quite a lot of time talking about it and its meaning. We concluded that this was not just a gift to convey thanks because of what was happening in the therapeutic work at that particular point. So it is worthwhile for the therapist to consider what feelings and thoughts are evoked by the gift. If it's not clear, then it's likely to be tainted in some way.

On the other hand, the therapist needs to be mindful if they ever think about giving a gift to a client. If this thought emerges, it deserves attention in supervision. It is likely that this has been induced by something in the therapy, probably coming from some developmental deficit in the client which has stimulated a desire in the therapist to give the client something other than what is given through the therapist's presence, attention and responsiveness.

Challenges of keeping relationships clear

The therapist needs to be mindful and think about the ethical implications of working with someone they may know in another context. This could prove to be very difficult in small, isolated, rural communities. A colleague I knew did see people from her village and surrounding rural areas. In this case the therapist had moved into the area so she didn't have a long familial history with the inhabitants of the area and she kept very good agreed boundaries if she bumped into a client socially. It's also important that the therapist has their privacy honoured as well! The extension of online provision has made it easier for people in remote areas to access psychological services without having to work with a therapist who may live in the vicinity.

Although living in a large town or city does not present the same kind of difficulties, it is possible that a client may live near the therapist, or the placement. Additionally, they may share a similar interest or have possible contact through a club or activity, e.g. bumping into each other at the tennis courts or the school gate. If the therapist thinks that there is a high probability of meeting outside it is worth discussing this with the client at the initial meeting. One way of doing this without disclosing your personal information is to pose the question, 'If we met outside the placement how would you like us to be?' This allows the client to indicate their preference about how they would like to be responded to. If there is any sign the client thinks the therapist might ask them how they are in the middle of the high street, allay their fears and make it very clear that there will be no personal therapeutic conversation with them. Alternatively you could make no arrangement and simply discuss it with the client if a meeting occurs. For a new trainee, guidance from your supervisor and measuring your own anxiety about the issue will help you determine whether this needs to be spoken about in advance.

Another element is created by what is known as having dual relationships. This is when you have or had a relationship with someone in an outside context – at work, at church, at a club, through membership of a group. It's clearer and more ethical not to take someone on as a client that you have known professionally or socially.

Challenges around social media

In our age of abundant social media, both the therapist and the client will have boundaries which need to be protected. For the therapist it is likely that a client will make a Google search before meeting them. Be aware of this: the therapist needs to know what information can be found on social media about them. Some of this information may not be under the therapist's control. However, professionally the therapist needs to take care what they post about themselves. There may be areas of the therapist's life that are not relevant to their current position, such as a former job or profession, memberships of groups or organizations and links with family members or friends which have no bearing on their new professional life. The wish to keep this information private helps to maintain a sense of therapeutic neutrality which is important for the work.

Technically proficient clients may find more information about the therapist and give a hint about this in the therapy room. If the client mentions they have seen a photo of the therapist on the Cats Adoration Society it is best to enquire about how this information has an impact on them – there is a meaning behind it – and if and how they think it will affect the therapeutic relationship.

From the perspective of the client I don't think it is appropriate for the therapist to pursue online searches about their clients. The main issue here is finding details about the client which may come from other sources and which may not be fully accurate. Thus some impression of the client is being put in the therapist's mind which unconsciously affects how they relate to the client in the room. Even if a client has posted the information themselves it will add to a sense of them, either positively or not. The therapist is now holding a piece of information from an outside source which was not brought explicitly into the therapy by the client. It is more appropriate to let the client reveal themselves, in their own time, in their own way, in the room.

The use of touch in therapy

Whether to ever touch a client in therapy is still a debatable issue within the profession. The formal handshake at the start and end of therapy is by and large viewed as being professionally appropriate, but beyond this there is a wide range of opinion about what might be a reparative action, an abusive action or a seductive response.

Trainee voice

'I would always shake a client's hand if it is offered to me, as to refuse it feels to me like a rebuke of the client for not "understanding" the counselling protocol.'

Here are some ways in which a therapist might touch a client, consciously or unconsciously. A therapist might:

- offer a hand to a client
- put a hand on a client's shoulder
- tap the client on the back
- put an arm around a client
- touch another part of the client's body
- hug a client
- inadvertently touch the client at some point, e.g. at the front door, or moving into the therapy room.

Self-reflection

1 *Which of the list of ways you might touch a client would you consider as appropriate therapeutic interventions and why?*
2 *Which of the above do you think your training organization would 'allow' or not 'allow'? What would be the arguments in favour of or against these actions from your training model?*

3 *If you have been in therapy, has your therapist ever touched you, and if so what was your response to this and why?*

4 *Here are two possible scenarios which may emerge in a therapeutic setting. Consider your theoretical and ethical position in your responses to them. The first is when a client asks 'Can I have a hug?' or goes to approach you with a view to making physical contact with you. How might you respond and why? The second scenario is when you feel so moved by the client's story and experience that you think words are not enough to convey your empathy to them and it activates an impulse in you to be physically closer to the client in order to take their hand or put a hand on their shoulder. How might you understand this impulse and how would you explain your action theoretically and ethically?*

It is as well to consider the possible meanings and implications of the use of touch in therapy in principle *before* it happens and through reflection in supervision *after* it has happened. Research discusses many aspects of the debate around this subject (Smith et al. 1998). Whilst body psychotherapists are specifically trained in the use of touch, most general training courses do not teach their trainees about the judicious use of touch in context. Some training programmes would give a clear indication that a therapist does not touch a client, while others may be more open to the use of touch in specific circumstances. It is certainly simpler not to touch a client, but whether it is always beneficial to hold this position is part of the continuing debate.

One of the key issues is centred on the debate about whether touch in therapy stimulates sexual feelings in one or both of the participants, which then may lead to the violation of boundaries. From the therapist's perspective, does the action of touching a client come from their erotic feelings that have been stimulated but that have not been acknowledged personally or thought about in supervision? Consequently, is the therapist wanting to touch the client because they feel aroused? Or has the therapist been unconsciously seduced by the client and is now responding by wanting to touch the client, and if so how do they want to touch their client? Is offering to hold a client's hand an erotic stimulant?

From another angle, if a therapist was motivated to comfort their client by holding the client's hand, would this intervention evoke erotic feelings in the client, and if so what are the consequences for the therapy? All of this is made more complicated because of how the client perceives and experiences the touch of the therapist. These can be muddy waters and what one party intends and means may not be what the other experiences. A colleague shared that they touched a distressed client's arm as the client was leaving the building, and in the next session the client said they nearly did not come back as they had felt sexually intruded upon. Fortunately the client was able to share his reaction and the two therapeutic partners were able to talk about what happened and what it meant for both of them. In this instance what was intended by the therapist to be supportive had created a rupture and it took a long time for the trust to be re-established.

Other points of the debate focus on whose need is being met by the action of touching a client. If the need is coming predominantly from the therapist it is likely to indicate that the content of the session is too emotionally demanding for the therapist to bear. In reaching out to touch the client the therapist is acting out of their feelings rather than containing them. So the 'comfort' in this case is actually for the therapist rather than the client. Another possibility is that the therapist has a strong 'rescuer' part (Karpman 1968) and cannot bear to see a client in pain, and too swiftly offers what they see as comfort to the client but in doing so inhibits the client from staying with their painful process. This interruption to the flow by the therapist's action may give the client the impression that they should not bring these feelings to the work.

Alyn (1988) makes a link between touch and power, suggesting that when higher-status individuals touch lower-status people, the latter are disempowered. This could be a danger in therapy because the client's vulnerability may make them feel less able to say 'no' to such an intervention. If the client has had a history of abusive touch in their life through sexual or physical violence it could feel very threatening or violating to the client and inadvertently retraumatize them.

Using touch is contraindicated if there is a poor working alliance and lack of trust in the therapy, or an unresolved rupture. If the therapist does not like being touched in their personal life it's not a good indication that the way they will offer touch to another will go smoothly and naturally. In addition, if the client is a 'secret' in some way, this means that the therapist has not brought this client to supervision or thought about their own deeper responses to the client. The latter may indicate that the therapist is hiding or avoiding some deeper response to the client. The danger is that without the support and the scrutiny of supervision the therapist may act unconsciously and impulsively in ways that take them to the edges of, or across, the therapeutic boundary.

On the other side of the debate the view is that appropriately touching another person who is in pain is part of a human instinct for healing that has been present throughout the ages. Historically many of the early analysts used touch to deepen the work. One of Freud's disciples Sándor Ferenczi argued that touch helped patients to contact deeper levels of pain than just talking (Smith et al. 1998).

In a study of 231 clients' responses to being touched, Horton et al. (1995) showed positive effects of being touched when built on a good therapeutic relationship and where both parties were able to talk about how they felt about it. There was relatively rare sexualized interpretation of touch.

If touch is being used it needs to be made as an offer to the client, e.g. 'I see your intense distress as you talk about the loss of your parent. I am offering my hand to you, if you want to take it.' Smith et al. (1998: 32) write, 'we suggest that touch may have a place in psychotherapy, but that its application requires careful thought, in-depth understanding of the therapist's own motivations, and a careful consideration based on the needs of the patient'.

The professional bodies, the UKCP and the BACP, do not specifically refer to the use of touch in their respective ethical code and framework. They do however talk about respect and not exploiting the client.

So key aspects to consider in principle would be:

1 Who initiates touch? Does the client make a request? Does the therapist touch without asking permission? Does the therapist ask permission of the client?
2 What could be considered as the benefit to the client if touch is used?
3 What is the effect of this touch on the therapeutic relationship? Does it help or hinder the relationship?
4 Do therapist and client have different perceptions of what the touch meant? Have these been discussed and clarified?
5 Can the therapist talk about touch with the client after this has occurred?
6 Is the touch planned or spontaneous?
7 How frequently does this occur? If this happens frequently, why?
8 Why is communicating verbally not enough? Not enough for which person?
9 Can the therapist talk about this intervention in supervision? If not, what might that mean?
10 How can the therapist account for using touch in terms of the theoretical model of practice they are being trained in?

I think if there are any doubts, then act conservatively and discuss what is happening in the therapeutic relationship in supervision.

Bending, breaking and avoiding boundaries in practice

In my experience as a trainer and supervisor, many new trainees find it difficult to maintain boundaries as they are over-sympathetic to the position of the client. So a 'rule/policy position' may slip or not be maintained. There may also be some anxiety in the trainee about confronting a client, so they avoid the boundary issue. I remember a trainer saying to me it is easier to start with firm boundaries than to begin with a more flexible approach and then have to strengthen the boundaries. On the whole training organizations and placements have spent much time considering policies and procedures in the interests of the trainee therapist, and of any potential clients. Boundaries have a useful rationale behind them. Boundaries create safety and are the markers and makers of ethical practice.

4 Supervision

Supervision: an essential ingredient

The Yale Book of Quotations gives an anonymous quote that says 'You can't make an omelette without breaking eggs.' Supervision at its best is a bit like making an omelette – something gets opened up, disturbed and then made into a new form. It feeds the maker and the receiver of the omelette when it is good.

I remember when I was a newly qualified therapist travelling nearly an hour and a half each way (no Zoom sessions in those olden days!) to see my wise, intelligent and compassionate supervisor who helped me feel that slowly I was getting there and could actually do it well enough. Three decades later I am still relieved after each of my individual supervision sessions that I have a strong, intelligent and highly ethically minded supervisor with whom I can talk about my professional practice. Overall, I have been very lucky that I have had for the most part very good supervision throughout my career.

Requirements for supervision

In the UK all registered practising therapists are required by their professional organizations to have a place of consultation or supervision which is additional to the therapist's own capacity to reflect on the work they do. The amount of supervision a therapist is either required or chooses to do depends on different factors. Whilst in training, therapists will be obliged to comply with the minimum requirements of their training organization (which are set by the awarding body and/or the professional organization the training course adheres to). Typically, training organizations require their trainees to work to either a ratio of 1:6 or 1:8 (supervision : client hours). The frequency of supervision is also stipulated. For trainees it is usually a requirement to present clients on a fortnightly basis in supervision so that there is continuity, which ensures that clients are discussed on a regular basis and that there is space and support for the therapist to talk about and reflect on the work they are doing. In the post-qualifying period the therapist has more freedom to decide on the amount and frequency of these sessions depending on their client load, as long as this complies with the minimum requirement of their professional body. For members of the BACP the current position (2022) is a minimum of 1.5 hours per month of supervision. For members of the UKCP the therapist will need to meet the requirements of their specific UKCP college.

Across-the-board supervision is regarded as an essential element in continuing to work professionally, and putting the client at the centre of the work. It enables the continuing development of a reflective and ethical therapist.

Supervision during training

For the trainee, the experience of being in supervision is often the bringing together of the theoretical framework, the ethical implications and the practical application of the work. Much growth and development in the trainee's practice comes from discussions and lessons arising from supervision. It is the setting where most discussion about the therapist and their client takes place; where the therapist can bring their concerns about how the work is going, get feedback on how to develop the work with the client and consider the elements that might trip them up with their client – their blind spots, their own material or countertransference (see below). The vast majority of the students I have trained have found supervision an invaluable asset for their development as a therapist.

Supervision formats

Training organization supervision

Training organizations want supervision to be in line with the core model of the course. To this end, many training organizations provide in-house supervision for their trainees with a supervisor who works with the core training model. If in-house supervision is not provided, the organization usually supplies a list of supervisors who are deemed to work in a way that is compatible with the training model.

The advantages of having in-house training supervision is that it helps the trainee by:

1 Sharing the same core theoretical ideas and principles of working with their supervisor rather than being in a supervision group with a different model(s) and maybe a supervisor whose emphasis on the work is very different from what you are being trained in.
2 Sharing the same terminology with their supervisor, which helps to avoid confusion about concepts and terms.
3 Belonging to a peer group who are at the same stage and level of experience, can create a sense of a 'level playing field'. There is a shared sense that we are all new to the work, all anxious and all eager to do well. This can create an atmosphere of peer support and encouragement.
4 Being within the net and network of the training organization, which can create a sense of a secure base to share and explore what is happening as clinical work begins.

Supervision in a placement

In addition to training supervision, therapists are likely to receive supervision in the clinical placement where they work – although a few do not offer this. In most cases supervision is free for the trainee, but as funding gets squeezed this may become less of a norm. If placement supervision is not offered, the therapist needs to know what supervision is required as a condition of their placement contract – e.g. the frequency of supervision, the modality and who will pay for it.

The potential benefits of having supervision within the placement are many. First, the supervisor will know, and therefore can support trainees about, any procedures the placement uses. This might feel particularly critical if the therapist is working with a suicidal client who seems to be in imminent danger. The supervisor is likely to have more local knowledge of the area, e.g. where other specialist services are offered and the availability of other support networks in the area. This information may be useful for clients who need either psychosocial support or input from statutory services, which will be additional to what is offered therapeutically. All of the above are useful if a client needs to be referred on for further work or support. Additionally the support through supervision and any other training input the placement offers adds to the sense of containment and security for the therapist. It also helps the trainee to feel part of a team or organization, which can be very helpful when starting out.

> **Trainee voice**
>
> 'Appreciate the "specialist" knowledge of the supervisors if your agency specializes in working with certain client groups, e.g. in a LGBTQ context: the supervisor will have a better understanding of the terminology and client experience than a more general supervisor, which is very supportive to both therapist and client.'

Challenges of being in supervision

There are some aspects of supervision that can create a challenge for the trainee regardless of the context of supervision (individual, group, training or agency). Much of this comes from the fact that the therapist has to show themselves and how they work to others. The private space of the therapy room is opened up in supervision. In addition, some training organizations require trainees to present recordings of their clinical work to the training supervisor. Inherent in supervision is the fact that someone else is keeping an ethical eye on the work and will give evaluative feedback about the therapist's professional development.

Fear of exposure

In order to learn and develop through supervision the trainee needs to be able to include all aspects of their work for discussion. This includes 'mistakes' the trainee has made or thinks they have made, their difficulties in the relationship with the client, their own difficult feelings about a client, which are often suppressed, elements of themselves they don't think match with being a 'good' therapist, and any procedural and contractual difficulties with their client. It takes courage to reveal these elements of the work and aspects of the therapist's self in supervision. Cooper (2008) cites research studies which indicate various ways in which trainees do not disclose all aspects of their work to their supervisor.

It can induce a degree of shame in the trainee to admit in supervision that something has gone wrong or that a mistake has been made. For some trainees, being in a group exacerbates these feelings as there are more eyes on them. All of this evokes complex internal processes in the therapist: their projections, assumptions and transference dynamics towards members of the group, most commonly the supervisor – for example, an aspect of the supervisor is (unconsciously) reminding the therapist of a teacher from their school life. If this was a challenging and difficult relationship in the therapist's early education some of these feelings and thoughts will be transferred to the new situation in the supervision room. If this dynamic is intense and persistent it makes being in supervision very difficult for the trainee. This can be exacerbated if the supervisor is asked to write a report on the trainee as part of either formative or summative assessment procedures, when feelings of being judged intensify. As well as making the learning experience difficult, this also impedes the learning process. Personal therapy is usually the best place to explore anything that has been evoked by challenging experiences in supervision.

On the other hand, I remember a time when I was a newly qualified therapist with a challenging client load, feeling very supported whilst returning home after supervision and feeling that my supervisor believed in me even though I felt I was struggling with some of the work. It does behove the therapist to bring as full a picture of their work – warts and all – to reap the benefits from supervision.

Trainee voice – starting supervision

'It's difficult to know what belongs in supervision and what belongs in your own personal therapy. I felt nervous to show any emotion in supervision because it felt like I was using the client's space for my own process. But when I let myself be moved it helped me realize something about what was happening with the client, and also release something that I was holding on to. I'm finding that the more honest and open I am in supervision, the more my clients will benefit (although it is difficult!)'

Aspects of competition

Competition between peers can be both spoken and unspoken within the group. Some trainee therapists need to show their knowledge and skills to others in a way that can come across as superior. This is often done unconsciously and comes from a narcissistic need in the therapist. If in addition this therapist is not open to the learning process it may lead them to cover up their own vulnerabilities and doubts about their work in order to maintain a sense of their own competency. While this inhibits the real learning of the therapist, it can also impact on the learning process and behaviours of other members of the group. Sometimes an obvious 'fight' could occur for supremacy of knowledge or to decide who is doing the 'best' work. If this dynamic goes unchecked it is likely to cause other members of the group to either compete or give up, especially if they are lacking in confidence at that time.

Another form of competition occurs if a trainee or member of the group competes with the supervisor. Whilst supervisors do not know everything, by virtue of their greater experience in the field they have accumulated some overall knowledge which is wise to listen to in the first place. If competition towards the supervisor turns into an inherent attack, members of the group will not feel safe to do the work they need to do.

Not getting needs met

Preparing for supervision by taking the time to consider what is needed from supervision is the basic starting position. Often trainees haven't done this and then can find supervision unsatisfying. Thinking about what 'I' need before supervision can be a useful investment for the therapist's learning. Over-compliance in supervision and allowing others to get their needs met is an aspect of self-denial or even self-sabotage. If this is happening it is useful to reflect on whether this is a repeated relational pattern or if it is triggered by the dynamics of the supervision group. Therapists may keep a low profile in a group by letting their client presenting time slip by, allowing other members of the group to always encroach on their time, being too quiet, hiding concerns about their work, especially if they are feeling vulnerable, or minimizing their needs in supervision.

Being in supervision and getting the most out of it means the therapist takes responsibility for their clinical needs. If this does not happen they need to reflect on what inhibits them from doing this.

Trainee voice

'Try to be clear about what you want from supervision. A place to start is to bring to mind all your clients – who surfaces first? Does this person always come to the fore? Are there other clients who do not come to mind readily?'

Challenges of being in a supervision group in a clinical placement

Most agencies offer group supervision. Some of the challenges associated with group supervision are:

1 The dynamics of inclusion/exclusion. It is fortunate if the therapist can join a newly formed supervision group which provides some degree of a level playing field, as all participants are starting together and in all likelihood with a supervisor unknown to all members of the group.

2 If a new trainee just starting in a placement is also joining a ready formed supervision group it can feel daunting. They don't know the client, the organization very well, their peers or the supervisor. This adds up to a lot of not knowing, which creates anxiety. This anxiety, however, is a normal feature of beginning something new and important, and hopefully abates once relationships are made and knowledge and experience gained.

3 How to feel included and valuable in the supervision group is critical for the therapist's ability to learn from being in the group. In this respect the supervisor does much to set the tone of the group in terms of creating a respectful and boundaried space in which all members can bring their clinical work for support, exploration, challenge and development.

4 Administrative difficulties. The supervisor is a representative of the placement and its management. So if things don't go smoothly this can create difficulties in the supervisory relationship. Administrative problems which the trainee can't fix may be brought to supervision with the expectation that the supervisor can and will sort them out. But in practice the supervisor may have little input or contact with the management of the placement to remedy the difficulty. So the fantasy of protection and support from the supervisor is diminished, if not ruptured. How the trainee can accept and deal with these administrative challenges is a mark of their growing maturity and capacity to sort things out for themselves by speaking to the appropriate person at the placement.

5 Differing developmental stages of clinicians. In a placement it is more likely that the group is made up of therapists from different stages of training or levels of expertise. This has both benefits and challenges. New trainees can learn a lot from listening to more experienced or newly qualified therapists. These group members are closer to the experience of the new trainee than the supervisor, who is the 'elder' or authority figure. The more experienced group members can act as role models for the newer trainee, which can be inspiring. Sometimes this doesn't work as well if a new trainee feels inferior or feels they are playing catch-up with the more experienced members of the group. This essentially reflects an inner process in which the therapist is caught in their own demanding, competitive or critical aspects of self. If this persists they will find learning in the group difficult. Another aspect of having group members at different levels of training is that each stage of a therapist's development stimulates different needs in supervision. Stoltenberg and Delworth's (1987) 3 Levels – beginning,

intermediate and advanced – identify some of the key processes, concerns and areas of interest for the therapist over their time in practice. The model recognizes that the new trainee has concerns about what to do and say to a client whilst needing a lot of input and support from supervision as they begin to learn what it means in practice to sit with and communicate with another person. Much of the supervisory input at this stage is about containing the anxiety of the trainee as they begin to settle into the work. A therapist at or nearing the point of qualifying, having gained some confidence in their ability to do the work, is able to consider more what happens in the therapeutic relationship, including the vital examination of their own processes and reactions. Then there is the long period of consolidation and mastering the art of the work post-qualifying as knowledge and experience are deepened and integrated. It is worth noting that at points of stress in the work or in the therapist's life, earlier developmental needs in supervision can be evoked even in very experienced therapists. There is no absolute linear progression, but there is an unfolding journey.

6 Different modalities of the participants. As many supervision groups in placements include therapists from different theoretical modalities, this can both enhance and enliven learning by offering a different viewpoint on human development and behaviour, and how to work with a client from a different perspective. A therapist from another modality may say something that shines a light in a different way on the client's process, which can be very interesting to hear and consider. Conversely, a new trainee could find these approaches destabilizing and confusing if they make the trainee question their own approach to understanding what is happening or what to do in the work. With growing experience of clinical work and increasing confidence in themselves to do the work, the balance between being reluctant to entertain a different view and being curious about it often shifts. After time this may allow the trainee to assimilate concepts outside their original training without feeling incompetent or conflicted. This is part of a wider process of integration that builds throughout a therapist's working life.

7 There is also the competitiveness that comes from a belief in one's own training model and approach being the best way – or at worst, the only way – to proceed in therapy. Certainty does create a sense of security, which may be important when starting out in clinical practice. However, if this becomes a point of conflict in the group it may add to the dynamics of superiority and inferiority between the participants, which needs to be managed by the supervisor. All of us harbour some degree of belief that what we have learned is best. In essence, what we believe in and hold on to is really best for us, suits us, fits us, at this point in time in our career. Hopefully as therapists develop with experience and become more open to other possible ways of working and ideas this tribalism diminishes.

8 Possible conflict between placement and training supervision. It is very difficult if the placement and the training supervisor have a different emphasis or opinion about a client. This can leave the trainee feeling conflicted or confused and even disloyal about having to abandon a particular supervisory

input. How the trainee makes a decision about what input to follow or how to reconcile what they see as different views calls on the trainee to trust themselves. This is a big challenge when starting out. Often trainees will make the decision on what to do or which way to go with a client depending on which supervision experience they prize more highly, or which supervisor/group seems to be more demanding, and which if not followed may lead to repercussions or difficulties with the supervisor. Sometimes the trainee will prefer and use the feedback which fits best within their comfort zone of competency at the time, thus choosing the interventions or focus in the clinical work which feel less challenging to try to implement at this point.

Trainee voices

'It is likely that whilst you are in training you may have two supervisors: one as your training supervisor and one from your placement. It can happen that you make one of them the "good" supervisor and the other the "bad" or "unhelpful" supervisor. It's important to be aware of this splitting and to think further about what is being triggered in you.'

'My two agency supervisors I have for different client groups and my college supervisor all have very different approaches, ranging from psychodynamic to person-centred. These diverse supervision perspectives teach me to trust my own judgement, encourage different ways of thinking about clients and allow me to develop my own unique "internal supervisor" with insights that are challenging and informative.'

All of this has to be considered against the background of who has clinical responsibility for the work – i.e. if things go wrong with a client, who is accountable? For the most part, placement providers accept and hold clinical responsibility for the work of the therapist as they have offered the service to the client. For this reason the trainee needs to be able to account for any actions suggested or signposted in placement supervision that they did not implement.

How to present a client in supervision

While it's true to say that each supervisor wants the therapist to present their client(s) in a specific way, taking into account specific requirements from the training organization, there are some general things that go across the board. Supervisors do need to have an overview of how the client presents themselves and responds in the therapy room, their present circumstances and significant events/experiences from their past. This overarching view helps the supervisor to gain a general sense of the client's life journey. Some supervisors want a short written outline of the client's history and present circumstances, to be provided to all members of the group before supervision takes place, whilst others are satisfied with an oral presentation in the supervision session.

Trainees get the most out of supervision if they have thought about which client(s) they want to talk about and have gathered clear information on the client:

1 Family history. Give some basic details about the client's age, the family or environment where they were brought up, their significant relationships and an outline of their education and work history.
2 Other significant experiences in life – either past or present – the highs and lows of the client's experiences including those related to the culture and society in which they were brought up and currently live in.
3 Current situation – including living circumstances, relationships, physical and psychological health, finances and work/study. Their sense of identity or conflicts about it.
4 Current or previous experiences of therapeutic or mental health interventions including medication.
5 Reasons for coming to therapy. What was the trigger for seeking therapy and have the original circumstances or issues changed?

All of the above information provides a narrative through which to think about the client and their life. If the trainee is stumbling to make a clear presentation of these details it gives an impression that care has not been taken to know and think about the client. These pieces of information set the scene and are the springboard for deeper discussion, debate and exploration in the supervision session. They are not enough in themselves.

For deeper exploration the therapist needs to ask themselves:

- What is my reason for presenting this client in supervision at this point?
- What is my hypothesis about the client?
- What am I finding challenging with this client?
- What am I feeling about this client – what do they evoke in me when I work with them?
- What do I think is happening between us in the therapeutic relationship?
- What do I think and feel have been less effective interventions and responses in the work?
- What have I been pleased about in the work so far?
- What might I want keep less in view about the client in our work?
- What help or input of ideas and techniques do I need to work more effectively with this client?

Not all of the above questions will be pertinent to the work with a specific client all the time, but they provide a broad scan for the therapist's consideration in preparation for supervision.

The relationship with the supervisor and the supervisor's style of work

Often when a trainee starts in clinical placement the supervisor can be seen as the 'all knowing' professional. There is a positive aspect to this fantasy in that it can create confidence in the trainee, who believes that if there are difficulties the 'all knowing' supervisor will actually know how to help them and know what to do about it. Conversely, the 'all knowing' supervisor might be an object of fear for the trainee, depending on their experience of authority figures. This will be intensified if the supervisor has to write a report for the training organization on the trainee's work, especially if this report is part of their qualifying assessment.

The style of the supervisor

All supervisors have their own style: some styles suit the trainee, while some may work less well. The working style of the supervisor in terms of how much support and challenge is given can have a huge impact on the trainee. New trainees do best if they receive realistic developmental support which gives them the sense of growing into the work.

Supervisors also come with their own theoretical modalities in place – humanistic, psychodynamic, existential, transpersonal or integrative. Generally, supervisors who work in a placement setting realize they are working with trainees of various persuasions and therefore temper their own theoretical approach in order to work in a more general way. However, supervisors do have a tendency to place different emphasis on areas of the work presented by the trainee or what happens in a group. The seven-eyed model of supervision (Hawkins and Shohet 2006), originally presented as the 'double matrix model' (Hawkins 1985), indicates that attention in supervision can be directed towards seven different aspects of the work presented. As a trainee it is not necessary to know this model in detail, but having a very basic outline of it may help to understand why supervisors place their attention and work in different ways.

The seven-eyed model identifies different foci or 'eyes' of the supervisor, which include:

- Finding out more about the client – their background and how they present to the therapist – what part or aspect of themselves the client brings to therapy (1st eye).
- Exploring what the counsellor says and does in the work with the client. This centres on the more explicit elements of what happens in the work (2nd eye). For a new trainee the above areas can be useful for discussion, guidance and support in supervision.
- Exploring what is happening in the relationship between the client and the therapist (3rd eye), including the implicit dynamics of the therapeutic relationship.

- Exploring the therapist's responses to the client (4th eye): what psychody-namic practitioners call the countertransference (see Chapter 10). This is a rich area to be deciphered, in particular by helping the counsellor to differ-entiate between responses they have to the client which are stimulated by their own inner processes, and responses in the therapist which are stimu-lated by an unconscious process in the client. Disentangling and shedding light on these complex inner processes requires honesty on the part of the therapist, especially if their feelings do not seem to fit with what the thera-pist believes they *should* feel about the client. This kind of deeper reflection on the part of the therapist, with the aid of the supervisor or supervision group, can be very illuminating. It is an opportunity to acknowledge and then explore the unconscious interpersonal communication between the two people in therapy and try to understand more deeply its meaning. Doing this is a very rich tool for helping the therapist to engage in and more fully under-stand what is being communicated between themselves and their client. Hawkins and Shohet (2006: 83) write, 'The goal is to enable the supervisee to surface unaware dynamics.' Casement (1985) gives a wonderful example of the complexity of this process in a case he supervised in his example 4.1.
- Giving attention to what happens within the therapist–supervisor relation-ship – the 5th eye. There can be lots of dynamics between the supervisor and the trainee: for example, in a supervision session the therapist is presenting their client in a way that makes the supervisor feel irrelevant – whatever the supervisor says or does has no impact on the trainee and the supervisor begins to feel left out. The supervisor realizes that this way of presenting clinical work is very different from what usually happens. So, being alerted that something is different, the supervisor can discuss this with the trainee and ponder with them if what is happening in the supervisory relationship is a clue to something in therapy, a likely understanding being that the client is keeping the therapist at bay in some way. This is what Searles (1955) identi-fied as 'parallel process', that is, what happens in the therapy between client and therapist is replicated unconsciously by the therapist in the relationship with their supervisor. When this is noticed in supervision it can provide a valuable insight into what is happening in the therapeutic process.
- Sharing what the supervisor is picking up (6th eye) and how this may relate to the work of the therapy.
- Considering the wider context in which the work is taking place (7th eye) and its impact on the therapy.

What is the supervisor looking for?

In essence, the supervisor is looking to see the therapist working as well as possible for their stage of development, remaining open to reflections on their work by bringing their successes as well as their difficulties and 'mistakes' to the supervisory process for scrutiny and contemplation. These actions demon-strate the therapist's willingness to move out of a narrative recounting of what happened in the therapy sessions with their client to really thinking about the work. It's the shift in the therapist from a defensive position of having it all sewn up for supervision to being able to unpick the cushion and see what's outside and inside it and the part they are playing in the work. Having opened up to discussion of their clinical work, can the therapist use the insights gained in supervision in the service of their client? This is best demonstrated by a capacity to reflect on feedback from supervision, learn from supervision and appropriately integrate new understandings and techniques from supervision into their clinical work. If too few of these things are taking place it means the therapist is either unwilling or unable at that point to use supervision as part of their professional support and development system. It is the responsibility of the supervisor to notice this, and to challenge the therapist about it.

Supervisors also notice the well-being of their trainee therapists as part of what Proctor (1987) calls the 'restorative' function of supervision. By allowing the therapist to bring the stresses of the work to supervision, some tensions can be discharged through the process of sharing the work. In addition, the supervisor often has a good sense of what the therapist is holding responsibility for professionally, and sometimes personally, and how these demands are balanced against the resilience and strength of the therapist. At times the supervisor has to suggest limits to the workload of the therapist, or discuss with them how they can improve their self-care in order to have the energy and resources to do the therapeutic work. These discussions are about the capacity of the therapist for self-care and self-support, and are intrinsically linked with maintaining standards of competency and ethical practice.

Feedback as part of the supervisory process

The primary purpose of receiving feedback in supervision is to assist the therapist to develop their competency and to maintain professional standards so that the client gets the best provision from the therapeutic service.

Receiving feedback and giving feedback as a member of a supervision group and/or training group are deeply relational and professional interactions which stimulate unconscious processes and create relational dynamics between the participants. If the therapist has a troubled history with 'authority' figures either in their own life story or from their training experience, it is likely that difficulties may occur when feedback is offered. All this is usually intensified at times when the therapist is stressed, or when formal feedback is offered either verbally or in the form of a supervisor's report.

The supervisor will be negotiating the balance of how much to support and how much to challenge the trainee at a particular stage of development. The cornerstone is the trainee–supervisor relationship, which revolves around how feedback is given and received, especially if the supervision contract stipulates some formal assessment of the trainee. It is likely that the training organization will require a report on the trainee at least annually in order to assess whether the trainee is suitable for continuing in training or ready to qualify. The therapist needs to make it clear to the placement supervisor what their training organization needs in terms of reports.

On an ongoing basis the trainee will be receiving input and feedback all the time. This is often not registered by the trainee, as it is not given in writing and is not delivered formally. This is a pity as trainees can miss the more subtle non-verbal affirmations such as nods of agreement made by the supervisor and their peers about their work. How this feedback is conveyed by the supervisor and peers, received and perceived by the trainee, and absorbed and integrated by the trainee is a complex process. Trainees are sensitive and vulnerable to feedback and comments on their work when they start (although this is also true at other points throughout their career) as they need to feel that they are doing a good, or good enough, job.

There is an art to giving feedback which hopefully will be modelled by the placement supervisors and course trainers. For feedback to be effective, it needs to be heard and thought about in the first instance. Feedback is difficult to assimilate and therefore use, if it is too much (quantity), not specific enough (quality), not related to clinical practice or too personal, or beyond the bounds of what is necessary professionally (irrelevant).

Starting with some of the 'too much' aspects, a therapist can be overloaded with feedback (usually not of the positive variety). It is therefore best to prioritize one or two points of feedback (even what you consider as positive feedback) rather than give a flood of feedback which is likely to be overwhelming. If one person in the group seems to get 'too much' feedback, it would be important to discuss what is actually happening in this situation. Is this scapegoating or is it a way for one person to take the limelight, or take the flak, enabling others to keep a low profile?

Feedback that is too vague, such as 'you have done great work with your client' or 'I would never do that with a client', without clarifying what is helpful or not, does not assist the trainee. Feedback that is focused on the person of the therapist without reference to clinical practice is likely to be experienced as a personal attack. These comments come through 'you are' statements as opposed to 'when you said this …', which are comments about the therapist's interventions. Generally, it is more useful to link comments to what is happening in the work.

These ways of giving feedback are often compounded in an unhelpful way because the timing of the feedback comes before some degree of trust has been built in the supervisory relationship itself. There can also be feedback that is 'too early' in the therapist's development or is alien to their training mode, which can make the therapist feel incompetent about their ability. All or some of the feedback 'statements' can have a deflating effect, and if this continues it saps the confidence of the new therapist and will close down their capacity to learn, reveal and explore in supervision.

Sometimes comments and feedback in supervision may be given in an appropriate manner but the therapist may still interpret them as negative. This does happen and it is unfortunate if this is not picked up for discussion. Whilst the supervision group is not a therapy space, sensitivity in picking up implicit dynamics is important so that the trainees can reflect on what is happening in the learning space.

Integration of supervision into clinical work

The Cambridge Dictionary (at dictionary.cambridge.org) defines integration as the way 'to become more effective'. I think this is a useful way of thinking about supervision input and how it is used to enhance the development of the therapist and the experience of the client. So what is brought together and how does this contribute to the process of integration?

In one way, the fact that the client material has been brought to supervision changes something already. The details of the client and the work are no longer solely in the therapist's head or in the therapy room. In supervision there is an actual and symbolic airing of the work which makes a difference by itself. Aspects of the work or the therapeutic relationship have been brought into the open. This can give the therapist another chance to think about their client and become more aware of something that was hidden or not given the weight it deserved. This can be as simple as the therapist hearing themselves say a word or give a description of the client that they hadn't paid attention to before. The therapist may notice a feeling or a body response become more prominent as they talk about their client, which needs to be discussed and understood. All of this new emerging information is taking place in the presence of another or others who are also experiencing responses to what is being presented. This is part of the richness to be gained in supervision – a colleague of mine described this as 'super-vision'. This acknowledgement of something that had been in the shadows, or even covered up, in the work is the first step to uncovering deeper meanings.

An example

In presenting their client in supervision the therapist inadvertently says 'he tightens up'. So the supervisor invites the therapist to explore the origin of this comment. Perhaps the therapist has felt this tightening up in their own body or it's their visual picture of their client. Maybe the supervisor had remarked about the therapist's body language as they were talking about their client, which then caused the therapist to make this remark. All of these possibilities are rich with potential connotations for exploration. Through the supervision session (or sometimes sessions) the therapist may become clearer about what the 'tightening up' might mean. Some possibilities are that this is an indication of the client's habitual alertness or anxiety. It could be that something in the therapeutic relationship is causing the client to feel anxious. Maybe the therapist is anxious but attributes this to their client.

Having discussed some ideas about what the 'tightening' may mean, the therapist then has to decide how, when and if these ideas are brought into the clinical work. This is what Woskett and Page (2001) call the bridge between the deeper understanding derived from supervision and what is taken out of supervision into the work.

Starting with how. If the therapist now thinks the client's physical response is a manifestation of their deeper experience, they need to consider how this hypothesis (it is still a hypothesis until it is verified by the client) is best given back to the client. Possible ways to do this include noticing and reflecting back to the client what the therapist actually sees physically, e.g. 'I notice that you tighten your face when you speak about ...', or 'I notice you tighten your neck and shoulders as you tell me about ...'. Then wait and see if the client can self-reflect on it. If the therapist becomes aware that this physical response is evoked at points of interaction between them, this could be given back in the service of exploring the relational dynamic between the two. Depending on training modalities, the therapist will offer this interpersonal comment in various ways, either by using the skill of relational immediacy (Culley 1991), such as by saying 'I notice you tightened your jaw when I said ...', or exploring unconscious dynamics by enquiring 'I wonder if you saw something in me as judging you, when I said I noticed you tightened your jaw?' (see Chapter 10).

When? It is generally inadvisable for the therapist to go post haste from supervision to delivering an intervention in the therapeutic arena. All insights and possible new directions talked about in supervision need some digestion time within the therapist so that they settle and refine within themselves. The therapist has to make these new understandings their own, so that they mirror their own language, rhythm and sense of professional self.

Trainee voice

'Supervision input does not need to be used straight away. Get the feeling for when the time is right. Supervision input and its input into the session needs to come from within the therapist rather than being a regurgitation of the supervisor's words.'

The other variable of when to do or say something entails the timing of the intervention. Good timing comes out of an evaluation of how much trust has been built within the therapeutic relationship and how ready the client is to use the intervention in order to self-reflect and self-challenge. The most amazing insight into the client and their process may emerge from supervision but its delivery into the work may be inappropriate or poor. If the trainee is feeling anxious they may push it into the clinical work rather than waiting for a more appropriate time. If this occurs there will be at best a clumsy intervention or at worst there could be a rupture with the client.

In the therapy room itself the therapist is negotiating within themselves the different positions of waiting, doing nothing or doing too much too soon.

When things go wrong in supervision

This happens when the professional and collaborative working relationship between the supervisor and therapist has been ruptured or has broken down. This rarely happens in one supervisory session but is likely to arise from a build-up of tension and difficulties in the relationship that have not been resolved.

One of the factors that makes the supervisory relationship complex and apparently contradictory is the role and responsibility of the supervisor. There is an inherent tension in the duty/tasks of the supervisor between being the facilitator of the therapist's professional development and career and their role/ function as a guardian of professional and ethical standards.

The main areas susceptible to stress in these relationships can be looked at from both viewpoints. For the therapist, particularly while in training or newly qualified, there is a natural need for support and validation about how they are working. So the therapist may have experienced too little encouragement for their work, or too much challenge or developmental feedback that they experience as criticism. All of these leave the therapist feeling unnoticed, not valued or punished. This may not have been the intention of the supervisor but if the effect of the supervisor's interventions are not helping the therapist to learn and develop as a practitioner, something has gone wrong between the two.

Supervisors also notice trainees who do not participate in the group or explore their therapeutic work on a deeper level. If this situation persists without either the supervisor or a member of the group bringing it into the open for discussion, the supervision sessions will turn into a 'getting through it' situation rather than a potential learning experience.

The supervisor's usual initial standpoint with new trainees is to accommodate as learning experiences the therapeutic omissions, slips, blunders or misunderstandings that are not helpful for developing the work. These happen all the time as part of the learning process and supervisors can use them to help the therapist to develop competencies and understanding through their 'errors'. However, the tension starts to mount when the supervisor can see no change in the trainee's practice and behaviour. The supervisor then needs to make explicit their concerns to the trainee (which may be done privately) so that the trainee has some time to change the way they are working. Giving time for the trainee to develop further and demonstrate their improved competency, ethical working practice and openness to learning is being fair.

If there are no signs of improvement the placement supervisor will discuss their concerns with the placement manager, who may have to give feedback to the training organization about the trainee. The training supervisor, as part of their contract with the training organization, would give feedback to the relevant trainers. To make a transparent system between the training organization, the supervisor and the placement there need to be clear channels for communication and an explicit statement that these lines of communication exist for feedback.

These tensions are exacerbated when the trainee needs a report from their placement supervisor, especially if this report is part of their evidence of competency in order to qualify. It is best practice for any report from the supervisor to be first shared with the trainee therapist rather than being sent directly to the training organization. This gives the chance for discussion about the comments between the supervisory participants, which is particularly important if this is a final report on the therapist's work. However, supervisors do have an overall ethical obligation as gatekeepers of the profession to voice their concerns about a therapist's fitness to practise, but this needs to be done so that there is time for the trainee to improve.

For the trainee, be clear about what is not working and what is needed in future supervision sessions, e.g. more support, more challenges, more time, if your allotted time is slipping away! To do this professionally and responsibly means not blaming anyone else for what has occurred. There is always the therapist's part in the process – either actively or compliantly! Having put these requests to the group, it's then up to the group and the supervisor to renegotiate the contract for the work.

Working to repair any difficult dynamics, helping trainees to extend themselves as practitioners and ingraining a sense of good ethical thinking and practice are all in the interests of the trainees' learning but are also crucial for the interests of the clients that are indirectly affected by supervision.

The diamond

Good supervision is a precious diamond in the 'training bag'. It provides a space to grow and explore in clinical practice; it provides a place of safety or a safety net when the work is demanding; it can be a place of support and cooperation, and it can imbue a sense of belonging to the wider professional world.

5 Working ethically and legally

Working ethically

Working ethically is the thread we weave throughout all elements of our professional life whilst in training and over the course of our careers. It's like the thread Ariadne gave to Theseus to help him find his way back through the maze after slaying the Minotaur. This ethical thread stems from our own value system and internal integrity in relation to how we see the work we do as therapists. The thread is also created and strengthened by our understanding of how to practise within the overarching framework or code of practice of the professional body we belong to.

The thread is what we hold within us all the time we work with our clients – often it is silently there emanating from our presence and put into practice through our responses and behaviours. At times the thread can feel scratchy and calls for attention. Looking at its shape we might find a knot, or loose or broken fibres in need of repair. This makes us consider what is 'right' or what is 'wrong' with the thread at that given moment and in that context, and whether it is guiding us appropriately.

What we see as morally right or wrong is influenced by the values that we hold as a society at a given time. We do not live in a bubble, and our own personal 'moral compass' is not the only guiding light for our decisions. So the relevant professional associations such as the BACP and the UKCP have provided frameworks/codes of ethics to guide their members. There have been regular clarifications and iterations of the ethical frameworks and codes, which have reflected the profession's change of emphasis and increased understanding about ethical issues over the decades.

Self-reflection – your value systems

1 *Consider your own value system: what is important to you and what do you value in your life? Having reflected on this, make some statements starting with 'I value ...' or 'I am committed to...'.*

2 *Thinking about the profession you are now training in, what are the values you bring specifically to your new profession? Make some statements starting with 'I value ...' or 'I am committed to ...'.*

3 *Looking at your answers to points 1 and 2 above, where do you notice any overlap and where is there a difference?*

History – latest ethical statements

Both the BACP Ethical Framework for the Counselling Professions (EFfCP) and the UKCP Code of Ethics and Professional Practice have been recently rewritten and published (in 2018 and 2019 respectively). When I finished my first training in Psychosynthesis there was a BAC (British Association for Counselling) but no psychotherapy organization until 1993. The BACP had a code of practice for its members, which remained in that format until 2002. Then there was a major overview and the code of practice was transformed into an ethical framework consisting of three main elements: the core values of counselling and psychotherapy, the principles on which these core values are put into practice and guide the profession, and the personal moral qualities of the practitioners that are needed to put the values and principles into action in clinical practice.

In the latest revisions of the EFfCP (2016 and 2018), whilst the core values, principles and personal moral qualities remain embedded and at the heart of the document, there is an additional section on good practice which is written in more definite terms. This change has come about for several reasons. First, there has been an increasing number of complaints against members of the caring professions in general, resulting in increased litigation. Also, the counselling and psychotherapy professions are not regulated by law, but are overseen by their own professional bodies. In a way we are an anomaly as we do not sit within the jurisdiction of the Health and Care Professions Council (HCPC) like other members of the psychological professions such as psychologists, counselling psychologists, and art, drama and music therapists.

The wording and spirit of the latest revisions are intended to bring the non-statutory counselling and psychotherapy professions more into line with the other regulated caring professions that are under the aegis of the HCPC. The new language mirrors the changes in intention and obligation towards our clients.

In the BACP's EFfCP (2018: 12, point 5) there is a definite spelling out of obligations for the profession. It states: 'We are fully and unconditionally committed to fulfilling a specific requirement of good practice where we state "we will" or "we must …".' At the beginning of its Code of Ethics and Professional Practice, the UKCP (2019: 1) states, 'As a practitioner you must …' and then lists the obligations and standards required for working ethically. Its language includes directives to the therapist to 'ensure that …', 'act in …' and 'not …' carry out certain actions that harm or exploit, or make or allow certain actions against the client's interests.

Reading and understanding the professional framework or ethical code to which you subscribe

Soon after the start of training, the ethical framework or ethical code which the training course adheres to will be read and discussed in the classroom. Trainees will also be required to become a student member of the relevant professional body. In joining a professional organization the trainee is agreeing to abide by their ethical framework or code. It's very important that the trainee has read and begun to understand what they are agreeing to ethically *before* they start clinical work. Reading these documents can be experienced as a remote or abstract exercise. However, when presented with a difficult experience or dilemma in clinical practice the framework or the code becomes an essential resource for helping to determine what to do in that situation – for considering what is right and what is in the best interests of the client. Supervision sessions are also occasions where ethical issues and dilemmas emerge from the work and where difficulties can be considered ethically.

Self-reflection

As you read the ethical framework or code in your training group, notice what resonates with your own value system for the profession. What do you think you will find easiest to uphold? What do you imagine might present challenges for you and why?

Considering yourself as a person, what personal qualities do you see in yourself that will support you in working as an ethically minded therapist?

Consider the following things that a therapist might say or think. What specific part(s) of the ethical framework or ethical code that you adhere to needs to be considered in relation to each of them? What is the more general theme or principle, including conflicting ones, relating to each?

- *I am too old to work as a therapist.*
- *I want to charge £150 per session.*
- *I am working with a client who lives two doors away from me.*
- *I made a terrible mistake with a client when I said ...*
- *I will encourage the client throughout their divorce proceedings.*
- *I asked my client for their mobile number for my records.*
- *I have just realized that I am going out with one of my client's cousins.*
- *My new client asked me if I was qualified.*

Key questions for thinking ethically

In practice the therapist needs to think about their behaviour and responses to a client – to have a capacity to ask and answer such questions as:

1 In these circumstances, what is in the best interests of the client?
2 Are there conflicting or competing ethical factors which I have to weigh up in order to act in the best interests of the client?
3 What are the difficulties I am struggling with as I weigh up these factors?
4 What or who could help me to weigh up these different factors?
5 What do I think are the consequences of my ethical decision – both in the short and long term – from the client's perspective?

6 How do I think my ethical decisions will impact the therapeutic relationship?
7 How might my ethical decisions have implications for the placement where I am working and for my own professional status/position?

Common areas of ethical consideration in practice

Risk assessment and emergency situations

In the training organization, placement induction or clinical supervision group there will have been discussions about the exceptions to confidentiality that are part of the contract with the client. The exceptions to confidentiality may be outlined in the literature of the placement as well, but they need to be reiterated by the therapist with the client at the first meeting (see Chapter 2). The client needs to know and agree to the point in the contract which explains that what they say is confidential, with the exception of times when there might be a risk of harm to themselves or others. If the client agrees to this, then in emergency situations it is easier to talk to them about the need to disclose something which is in the interests of their safety. If the therapist has not already mentioned this exception to confidentiality it can create a very difficult ethical dilemma/conflict for the therapist about having to break confidentiality if an emergency situation arises.

If a client is expressing serious suicidal intention and has a plan to take their own life but is refusing to accept any additional support which is suggested – e.g. enlisting the help of their GP or being willing to go to A&E for an emergency assessment – the therapist is immediately placed in the dilemma of whether to respect the autonomy of the client or to take action on their behalf. In a placement setting there should be a senior member of staff to share this dilemma with or someone who is accessible quickly by phone, such as a senior manager or a supervisor. I know of no supervisors who would be annoyed with a trainee calling for help and support in these circumstances.

All the tension surrounding an emergency situation is exacerbated when working with a client online. If they are refusing to get any further support the therapist could (if they know the client's address) call the police and ask them to make an emergency visit to the client's home in order to help them access further mental health support – though of course the client may not be there. Being explicit and clear at the beginning of the work about the limits of confidentiality is therefore very important.

Consider this specific dilemma: if a client tells you that they have just seen their partner take a bottle of pills, where does your ethical obligation lie?

Boundaries outside the therapy room

Boundaries need to be clear and strong, but sometimes they can become unclear or messy.

Self-reflection

You have been seeing a client in private practice for some time. It has become apparent that the client sings in the same choir as a close friend of yours and knows your friend quite well. Up to now you have kept this knowledge to yourself, and your friend does not know that their friend (your client) is seeing you professionally. Therefore up to this point it has not created any difficulty in the therapeutic work. Your friend then tells you that she is going to invite the choir to sing at her wedding, to which you will also be invited. The invitations have not been sent out yet.

So what are the ethical issues emerging from this situation? How would you decide what to do ethically and how might you think and feel about your decision?

Competency

When I did my mental health placement in a psychiatric unit, the consultant psychotherapist who interviewed me for the placement asked me quite directly who he should *not* refer to me as a client. (I was going to see some clients as part of the placement.) I was quite surprised that I had been asked this question. After some reluctance I did say that it would be best not to refer to me anyone who had abused young children. This was a difficult question for me as I wanted to feel that I was open to working with anyone who sought help, but the question did make me think again at a deeper level. That was my position at the time – largely due to the circumstances in my life at that time. It's not an answer I would give now. I am, however, very glad that I was invited to think about it and to honestly admit my position.

The following is an example where supervision brought to the fore some ethical difficulties. The trainee had been working in a placement for over six months with a client who had a complicated history with a lot of neglect, a current situation which had many problems including social ones, and an eating disorder which was only becoming apparent as the client revealed more of her story. The client was also quite alone and unsupported in her life. The therapeutic alliance she had made with her therapist was very significant for her. The trainee therapist had done well, providing a basis of trust and safety for the client, and making a genuine and heartfelt commitment to her. The therapy was mainly of a supportive and containing nature for this vulnerable client. However, the client was very needy and anxious – she would often ring the service reception between the weekly sessions, checking the time of the session (which never changed), having a query about the payment of her fee, making admin enquiries or requests to give her therapist a message. On one occasion when the client was in the waiting area there was an incident which brought her to the attention of the counselling service manager as well. The manager began to realize that the client was not an appropriate fit for what the service could offer. This led to the placement supervisor making some comments about referring the client to the mental health team and getting additional social support for her. When the trainee went to her training supervision group she expressed her great distress at feeling she was being advised to give up her client. Discussions in her training supervision group did not easily abate her concerns about what needed to happen in the best interests of the client. The trainee was very torn by having to ethically balance what she believed was the usefulness of having an established and trustworthy therapeutic relationship with her client, and a disruption through ending the therapeutic contract and referring the client on to an unknown new team. It was very painful for this new trainee to relinquish her client and to do it in a way that did not make the client feel inadequate. The trainee therapist had to find a place inside herself that could accept the reality that the client's best interests would be served by making a referral to other services.

The therapist's well-being

I remember a colleague of mine telling me about how she had to challenge another colleague in a peer supervision group about the quality of her work. They knew each other quite well as they had been in the same supervision group for some time. On one occasion, after much mental torment about whether she should say something or not, my colleague decided to express her thoughts and concerns about how her peer was working and the standard of her work. Her peer then admitted that she had come off her long-term medication for a physical condition as the medication was not suiting her. She was initially distressed by this challenge, but grateful to have the feedback about her professional practice, and took steps to restore her health and the standard of her professional work.

From this anecdote the question arises: how do I know if I am well enough at any given point to work in clinical practice? Balancing the stressors in your life, particularly whilst you are in training, is also related to this question (see Chapter 7, 'The presence of the therapist').

Trainee voice – a difficulty

'I was surprised by how difficult I found it not being able to talk to my usual support network (husband, friends, family) about client work. I speak about how client work is impacting me in supervision, personal therapy and within the training group but it's hard having to establish a new support network, and also having a gap in what I can share with the people closest to me. I didn't expect that.'

Ethical working in relation to legal issues

What we see as 'right' or 'wrong' is not always the same viewpoint as what is upheld by the law of the land. Sometimes an ethical response and a legal requirement fit together; at other times they are different or in conflict. The UKCP Code of Ethics and Professional Practice (UKCP 2019: point 33) states that the therapist must 'maintain an awareness of, and comply with, all legal and professional obligations'.

There may be a conflict between ethical and legal positions. For example, is it permissible to have a sexual relationship with a client? The law could take the view that two consenting adults have made this decision – unless the client was deemed to be a vulnerable adult (see below) – but ethically it would be seen as exploiting the therapist's position of power, breaking trust and breaking the therapeutic contract.

Under the Protection of Vulnerable Adults Regulation 2002, a person over 18 who may need community services because of a disability, age or illness and who cannot look after or protect themselves is regarded as a vulnerable adult. Also, people who have been diagnosed with a physical or mental illness or have an addiction to alcohol or drugs may come into this category. A key consideration for vulnerability is reduced physical or mental capacity.

The other major consideration which comes in to play is: when does the legal requirement take precedence over any ethical position we may hold? The BACP EFfCP (2018: 13, point 9) states, 'We will give careful consideration to how we manage situations when protecting clients or others from serious harm or when compliance with the law may require overriding a client's explicit wishes or breaching their confidentiality.'

Jenkins (2007) identifies three factors which affect the therapist's relationship to the law. First is the *context* in which the clinical work takes place and if the context of the work involves statutory obligations. In essence, what are the legal implications for working in a voluntary placement, a placement that has funding from the public purse, and/or what are the implications for private practice? Second is the *client* group you are working with – e.g. vulnerable adults, a special group or children – and third, the therapist's *employment* status – i.e. voluntary, employed or self-employed.

Laws most likely to impact practice

The Data Protection Act 2018, which implements the General Data Protection Regulation (GDPR). This was designed to develop a culture of transparency with regard to the records that are kept on people. Jenkins (2007: 131) defines data in this context as every piece of information related to 'an identifiable living person'. This data can be electronic or handwritten. Most therapists will have some electronic data on a client, e.g. a mobile number or perhaps an email address. This means the therapist is considered a data handler and will need to register with the Information Commissioner's Office (ICO).

Children Act 2004. At present in the UK there is no mandatory obligation for *all* professionals to report abuse against children. Some professionals are bound to do so by the terms of their employment. So if a therapist is working in

Child and Adolescent Mental Health (CAMHS) or for social services or in a school they will be legally bound to report abuse to the safeguarding officer or team.

Sexual Offences Act 2003. Under this Act it is a criminal offence for a person in a position of trust to engage in sexual activity with a person under the age of 18. An example would be a teacher engaging sexually with a pupil aged under 18. What also needs to be kept in mind is if young people are engaging with teenagers where there is very little age difference, e.g. a slightly older teenager of 17 may be a team leader with 16 year olds. If they have a sexual relationship, the 17 year old would be considered as abusing their position of trust.

For therapists working in private practice there is no legal obligation to report abuse but many therapists believe they have an *ethical* duty to do so.

Self-reflection

A client who is now a young adult and seeing you in your placement tells you that their grandfather sexually abused them as a child. The grandfather is still alive and you know he is in contact with other young members of the family, and your client has serious concerns for their safety.

1 *What would you do?*
2 *Do you have enough information to act on?*
3 *In whose best interests would you be acting?*
4 *What relative weight should you give to ethical as opposed to legal obligations in this instance?*
5 *What might be the consequences of your action?*

Hearing about suspected child abuse is very stressful for the trainee. It is therefore very important to talk to your supervisor or placement manager/safeguarding officer in the first instance. Do not take further action without the advice of someone more experienced unless there is immediate danger to the client or another person. The therapist needs clear practical details of the circumstances where there might be harm to a client or another person – often the therapist does not have this information. If a client gives details about a child they know who might be in imminent danger, the therapist could contact the local child protection team, the social services emergency duty team or the police. It is better to talk to the client about this. If the client is an adult, help them to make a decision about the information they have given about the situation – it is best if the client can act on the knowledge with your support.

Adoption and Children Act 2002. There is another issue about working with children that may come your way in practice. It comes from an amendment to the Adoption and Children's Act of 2002 which states that a therapist who is working with a client directly about their adoption issues must be employed by an adoption agency or an agency registered as an Adoption Support Agency

(ASA). In essence, they must be an Ofsted-registered adoption counsellor. The dilemma for therapists is that specific issues around adoption may not have been what brought the client to therapy, and if the therapeutic relationship has developed well, referring the client to another practitioner could be very detrimental. Stephen Hitchcock (2022: 50) in *Therapy Today* cites Ofsted (2021): 'You do not have to register if an adoption related issue only emerges after counselling begins and is not the primary concern or focus.' It is best to advise the client that they have the right to access specialist support, so there should be a discussion about what is in their interests in terms of the focus of the work and what choice they want to make about their therapy.

The Prevention of Terrorism Act 2005. This Act makes it an offence to know about an act of terror and not report it to the police or appropriate authorities. Since July 2015 there has been a statutory duty for specified authorities to prevent people from being drawn into terrorism, which is known as the Prevent duty. The placement or training organization may require that this online course on Prevent training is completed.

The Money Laundering Act 2017. This Act makes it a criminal offence if a therapist does not disclose information they have acquired in the course of their professional duties about money laundering for terrorism.

Use of language in clinical notes

If a client reveals a serious event or ongoing experience in their life (present or past) this will need to be recorded in the clinical notes and/or the notes kept by the placement. The information needs to be written using the words of the client – a narrative account, with no comments by the therapist. This is the clearest way to record this information should the clinical notes be requested for legal purposes.

Requests for information

Trainee voice – request for report

'I was asked by a client to write a short report of her progress in counselling to support her in an employment tribunal. With the support of supervision, I learned how to maintain the boundaries of confidentiality, as well as how to balance the wishes of the client, my agency and ultimately myself. In the end, reflecting with the client on how she herself felt she had progressed in our work together, asking her to write the report from her point of view, and then working together on a succinct version that my client and I, as well as my agency, agreed could be passed on, proved instrumental to our work – as did giving my client agency to decide whether she wanted to submit this report or not. It became a powerful mechanism for the client to appreciate her progress and exercise her own choice over the progress of her case, and how much of her personal progress she ultimately wanted to disclose.'

There is no 100 per cent confidentiality in terms of the law. A therapist cannot refuse to submit their client records on the ground of confidentiality. There are certain circumstances under which you cannot refuse to disclose your client records. This happens if you receive a letter from a solicitor or from the police with your client's consent or a subpoena from the Court.

If you do have to submit your records, only give a copy of the sections that are relevant to and provide evidence for the case. This maintains the confidentiality of the other parts of the client's history. For more on this see Mitchels and Bond (2010), *Essential Law for Counsellors and Psychotherapists*.

The impact on the therapist

Being faced with a situation or dilemma that has ethical or legal implications is usually stressful for the therapist. Taking support from the placement supervisor is the first step. There is also the ethics committee or legal team of your professional organization who can be contacted for information or advice. These dilemmas on the whole are better resolved with measured consideration behind them.

6 Assessment in training

The thought of being assessed during counselling or psychotherapy training frequently creates a sense of foreboding if not trepidation. I remember in the last year of my Psychosynthesis training receiving some very robust feedback from one of the senior trainers after a skills session. I went home very despondent but after the initial emotional response felt very determined to make use of the feedback in my practice. It is ironic that the very last observation on my skills was given by the same tutor, who then affirmed that my way of working was very different from what she had seen at the beginning of the training year. Take heart when you don't hear what you wish to hear from your tutors. Usually there is a gem somewhere in the feedback that is valuable for you.

Professional terminology

All training courses have different ways of assessing a trainee's work. A student handbook from the training organization should contain an overview of what is expected in each training year and the assignments for the year. For clarity here are some key terms used by training organizations and professional bodies.

Qualifications – certificates, diplomas and degrees

These are the formal documents which prove that the therapist has successfully completed a course of study and has passed all the requirements set by the training organization and the external awarding body or university associated with the course.

It is also important to note that professional bodies such as the British Association for Counselling and Psychotherapy (BACP) and the UK Council for Psychotherapy (UKCP) do not award qualifications to individual therapists. They validate training courses as having met the standards for counselling or psychotherapy training.

Internal and external assessment

Turning to the specifics of training: courses have internal and external elements of assessment. Internal assessment consists of all the work which is being marked by members of the tutor team from the training organization. Typical of this are essays, case studies, reflective writing, assessment of skills, supervision reports and reflections on clinical practice. These will make up the portfolio of work.

All training courses now have some items of the trainee's work which are externally assessed or marked by members of the training organization who have not taught the trainee. The purpose of this, which is a good one, is that a boundary is maintained. If the examiner or marker does not know the trainee they are impartial when assessing the work. Often the examiner/assessor is only given a number for the work to be assessed so the trainee can be confident that there is no bias in the marking. In a broader context, external examiners for awarding bodies may be assessing the work of trainees from various organizations, so they have in mind a standard which needs to be met for all candidates who are completing a particular qualification level. This provides the means to standardize levels of competency across various courses in different organizations which are offering the same qualification.

External assessment of skills can be through:

- the submission of a recording and transcript with a client or peer whose permission has been gained and whose personal details have been protected
- a live session with a peer or trainee from a different group.

The examiner in all cases will be looking to see that the therapist is demonstrating their capacity to work within the training model of the course.

External assessment of theory into practice can be through:

- the submission of a specific piece of work, for example a case study
- undertaking a formal written examination
- the submission of a dissertation
- a viva examination.

On longer courses – usually psychotherapy training – part of the final assessment is a viva voce exam, where candidates present their work to an examination board of about three or four senior psychotherapists or trainers. The therapist will be asked to demonstrate their model of working to the examiners, who will be looking for depth and accuracy of knowledge, clear ethical practice, an ability to understand and work with cultural diversity and difference, and the ability to work within a consistent theoretical model. The trainee may be required to present a segment of recorded clinical work for discussion and scrutiny. This is a strenuous and demanding examination.

Whether for internal or external assessment, training organizations should prepare and advise their candidates about the criteria against which the examiner will be assessing their work. Trainers also need to ensure that therapists who are not ready to undertake assessment, especially external assessment, are not entered for this and are given recommendations and/or additional time to prepare for a later examination date. Trainees are also part of this evaluation system as they consider their own readiness to be put forward for final assessment.

Formative and summative assessment

Black and Wiliam (1998) refer to 'the medals and missions' of feedback. The medals are the praise and positives of the therapist's work in the present; the mission is the feedback about what still needs to develop in the therapist. To this end, training organizations give both formative and summative feedback.

The Glossary of Education Reform (2015) defines formative assessment as methods that help teachers to evaluate whether a student is comprehending key concepts, acquiring the appropriate skills and making progress to the required standards at that point in their training. In general, this is feedback about how the therapist is working and developing as they go along. This formative feedback may be informal – for example, a brief comment from a tutor or supervisor such as 'that was a clear presentation of your work with your client' or 'in this skills practice I can see how you have improved your ability to challenge a client'. These comments are often verbal remarks made in the moment, and sometimes trainees do not pay enough heed to them as they are not written down. This is a pity because they are intended as a source of encouragement for the trainee and to offer pointers for their development.

In the theoretical, research and reflective elements of the course, feedback from tutors is written and formative. The purpose of these comments is to help the therapist develop their thinking capacity – especially critical thinking – reflect on how theoretical knowledge is linked to clinical practice, and develop a deeper reflective capacity about their own personal and interpersonal processes. If an assignment has been referred or has failed, the tutor comments need to clarify what is needed in order to resubmit this work and the time frame for making a resubmission.

At various points in training, usually the end of each year, all components of the trainee's work – theory, skills, clinical work and overall development – will be reviewed by the training team. These reviews will determine whether a trainee continues into the next training year or whether they have already successfully completed the entire course and are ready to qualify. In other words, this point is a general summing up on the training journey. There is often some written summative feedback at this point.

Common challenges for trainees concerning assessment

1 If the trainee has a demanding critical inner voice it can make formative feedback very difficult to hear and assimilate as something that is intended to help their development. Instead, the feedback may be turned against the self, thus starting a negative and possibly despairing cycle.
2 If the above happens a trainee may feel shame. Mollon (2002: 25) writes that 'Shame is a response to failure and to ensuing feelings of inadequacy – especially a failure when success was expected. Such instances always

involve a sense of failure in the eyes of others.' Assessment provides ample opportunities for a trainee to experience this if shame is a hidden vulnerability within themselves. It could lead to hiding aspects of their work or themselves from their trainers and peers. This stops or reduces the real opportunity to learn.

3 Trainees who have dyslexia or another neurodiverse presentation can find written work very challenging.

4 Tutors may be turned into 'bad' people and this can get stuck in the relational dynamics so that any 'positive' feedback on work is given no weight or is not heard and registered.

5 Giving and receiving feedback from peers. Developing the skill of giving feedback to peers and the capacity to receive and evaluate feedback from tutors, supervisors and peers is another aspect of professional development. See Chapter 4 on supervision, which has guidance about giving feedback.

Trainee voices

'I have learned to let go of perfectionism! While my pride can find this difficult to say, having to look again at a referred assignment has really deepened my learning. I am asked to think deeper – about myself, my client, my own material and how that is affecting the therapeutic relationship. While this is a test of spirit and resilience, I can feel it making me a more reflective, self-aware and, ultimately, a better counsellor.'

'The thought of assessments was nearly enough to stop me doing the course, especially the thought of a skills assessment. For me, it was another opportunity to be judged and criticized by someone in power, to tell me I'm not good enough, so why put myself through that. But I'm so glad I did. I learned that I didn't need to be perfect, that people didn't laugh when I made mistakes, and when I do make mistakes the self-learning is so much greater. I still don't relish skills assessments, but I no longer feel the familiar rise of panic and fear. Instead, I am able to trust that I am good enough. The support offered by peers and my tutors has been so deeply reparative – a safety net ready to catch me.'

'I would specifically like to address any new students coming on to a counselling course who are neurodiverse. In my first year, I was having real difficulties every time I was given an essay. I didn't understand why, I felt I wasn't good enough and had a lot of self-doubt. My tutor noticed that there was a significant difference between how I contributed in class and my written ability. This triggered a Needs Assessment and weekly Adult Learning Support with a dyslexia tutor. Experiencing such support has been motivating and enabled a shift in my thinking. This has allowed me to notice and value my strengths, and give myself permission to learn. I am still a work in progress but I faced every assignment and found a way through.'

The main components of assessment

Trainers want to see how the trainee works to an appropriate standard as a clinician, how they explain and analyse their understanding of human experience in accordance with the course model, and how they demonstrate a robust, reflective and ethical presence both within the training organization and in their clinical placements.

In terms of skills and clinical competency, the main vehicles for feedback and for formative and summative of assessment include:

1 Observed sessions in the training room. Trainees start in their foundation year or first year of training by practising skills with their peers in pairs or in a group of three (sometimes called a triad) – counsellor, client and observer roles. These short skills lab practice sessions usually last about 10 to 15 minutes but increase over time. Additionally, there may be what are called 'goldfish bowl' sessions where trainees take on the role of therapist and client and do a session in front of the whole training group (or divided training group). This can be challenging, especially in a new training group and in the presence of a tutor. After these sessions it is usual to have a discussion in the group, which will include comments and observations about what happened in the session, for instance about what was happening in the therapeutic relationship, processes which emerged in the session, or the effectiveness of the therapist's responses to the client. These discussions in the group can be very informative for the therapist and the other members of the group. There will also be evaluative feedback about what went well, what did not work so well and what might need to be developed in the therapist or included in future work, and how far the therapist was working within their own training model.

2 A recording or part of a recording with a verbatim transcript and commentary from the recorded session with a peer or a client (if this has been agreed with the placement agency and the client). Initially, these transcribed sessions can be very daunting to listen to. Many trainees cringe when they hear themselves on the recording for the first time. This is because the trainee is very visible in the recordings and every intervention and response they make is under the microscope. The purpose of this is to give very specific feedback to the trainee about how they are working with a client. Listening very carefully to these recordings and discussing the trainee's interventions and responses can be a very rich source of learning about how the trainee communicates and their technique. It helps the therapist to reflect upon why they made that specific response at that point in the session, and if it hindered or distracted from the clinical work. Note: this scrutiny also shows what the therapist did well! A recording can also reveal aspects of the therapist's own processes whilst they are working. For example, if the therapist has failed to pick up a fleeting comment about a client's experience of bereavement this may be an indication that the therapist has some unresolved personal material around loss which they were unaware of. Overall, I

believe listening to and reflecting on the segment of the session with such a fine-tooth comb can be a very rich source of learning and therefore potential development for the trainee therapist.

Key elements to demonstrate clinical competency

In terms of being able to demonstrate clinical skills competency over time, trainers will be looking for the therapist's ability to:

1 Hold a therapeutic presence and make psychological contact with the client. They want to see that the therapist can maintain a sense of their own self whilst working but also have the capacity to be open to the client.
2 Maintain boundaries within the session and beyond. This involves making a contract for the work which sets out the time boundaries of the session, the confidentiality contract and the therapeutic contract which clarifies what the client's needs are for the specific session.
3 Respond to the client's explicit narrative and emotional language. This creates a sense of safety which will facilitate the work to a deeper implicit level.
4 Pick up and reflect back the client's implicit narrative and emotion through the therapist's ability to attune to the client (Stern 1985/2000), demonstrate empathic responsiveness (Rogers 1951/1957), pick up the deeper meanings or the ability to appropriately offer an interpretation (Howard 2010). These attributes demonstrate the therapist's capacity to work with deep unconscious emotional processes in the client and to be a container for them. This is critical for helping the client to see what is hidden within and to face it in the presence of another.
5 Work with other implicit processes, e.g. the client's non-verbal communication, their use of metaphor or what they allude to. Points 4 and 5 are major components of what the trainers will be wanting to see demonstrated in the practical work. Also see Chapter 9, 'Working with feelings'.
6 Appropriately use themselves and what they are picking up to respond to the client (Casement 1985) (Howard 2010).
7 Enquire about and challenge the client's assumptions and fantasies in order for the client to understand themselves better.
8 Work with the relational dynamic between therapist and client. The trainee needs to show how they respond and work with the dynamics, difficulties and challenges of the therapeutic relationship in ways that are appropriate to their core model. Also see Chapter 10, 'Working with the therapeutic relationship'.
9 Demonstrate your capacity to work with issues of difference and diversity in an appropriate way.
10 Use techniques and methods congruent with the training model. Trainers need to have clarified any specific skills they want to see demonstrated in skills practice and particularly in any final formal assessment.

11 Show in discussion afterwards a capacity to reflect on the session – why interventions were made and their effectiveness, what could have been done differently, how ethical issues were acknowledged and attended to, the impact of difference and diversity on the relationship and other dynamics in the therapeutic relationship.

As a general rule of thumb, trainers don't want to see:

1 The overuse of questions which are likely to keep the session at a narrative or cognitive level.
2 Inappropriate self-disclosure which is likely to distract the client from their own story. Note: self-disclosure must always be in the interests of the client. If you have any doubt about sharing your experience with a client, it is best not to do it.
3 The overuse of psychoeducation explanations.
4 Fixing or prematurely closing down a client's process through giving advice, or rescuing a client from difficult and painful experiences and processes – what I call 'pink bow' interventions.
5 A therapist who can't cope with the material which has been disclosed, for example by becoming overwhelmed, or a therapist who colludes with the client because they have lost their own sense of presence and capacity to think.
6 A punishing, attacking or over-directive therapist, which indicates some form of unethical practice.
7 A lack of capacity to reflect on the work.

The importance of theoretical understanding and putting theory into practice

The purpose of theory can be more difficult to place within the context of a practical therapeutic relationship. The main reason courses include theoretical components is to broaden the trainee's ideas about how human beings are formed psychologically and to offer other viewpoints about human behaviours and responses. Learning about the ideas and discoveries of other clinicians and researchers broadens knowledge by offering perspectives other than those which come from personal experience. Thinking about theory can be stimulating and rewarding but also challenging, especially if the trainee is attached to certain ideas that they have held for a long time.

Theoretical understanding gives the therapist a rationale so that they can explain how and what they do, in order to be accountable for how and what they do. A theoretical map can be shared with other professionals, whether they are peers, supervisors or trainers. In many clinical placements trainees find themselves in a mixed-modality group for supervision and need to be able to talk about their practice and the thinking behind it.

It quickly becomes clear to the new trainee that working with clients is very demanding. In the room they are in the heat of the relationship with its varying dynamics. If there is a lot of emotion in the room, either explicitly being expressed or unconsciously being transmitted, the therapist can feel overwhelmed, unsure of what is going on, not clear about what belongs to the client or what belongs to their own process. Having a theoretical map helps the therapist to understand the client and what is happening in the therapeutic relationship, which is like having some scaffolding to hold onto in the room and afterwards. If we had no theory or only our own self-constructed model of a person, we could be lost in the sea of emotion.

If, for example, a client is very upset about the therapist taking a break, having a theoretical framework could help the therapist to understand what is happening to the client in response to the break. The therapist no longer has to work with what was known in early aviation parlance as 'flying by the seat of the pants' – i.e. responding always through instinct.

Theory helps the therapist to keep steady when exploring deeper layers. I am not suggesting that the therapist should be giving major attention to theory whilst they are with a client, as this would be distracting from what is actually happening with the client. However, after the session and in supervision, discussion of theoretical ideas can help the therapist to make sense of the session and the dynamics within it.

Theoretical ideas can help with seeing a way forward for the therapy – for some training programmes this is regarded as part of the clinical formulation and treatment planning for the work. Thus thinking about the client – making a hypothesis about their core psychological wounding, their experience of relationships, their basic difficulties and challenges in their current life and what is emerging (or not) in the therapy room – can encourage thinking about what else might be needed in the therapy as it moves forward. Note: this does not mean having a rigid idea about a client or sticking to a rigid plan for the course of the therapy.

Over time, and not just during the period of training, the therapist will begin to assimilate and then integrate knowledge and ideas that make sense for their practice as a clinician. In the therapy room, theory is not to be imposed on a client in the guise of therapeutic intervention; rather, it is to be used as an aid to help unravel the mystery of the person who is sitting in the room and who is struggling to articulate and alleviate their own distress.

Be theory-held, not theory-led!

Assessment of theory

Key words used in assessment

This section introduces some key words used in theoretical assignments. Below is a short scenario which is used as a base to illustrate how to apply some of the key words used in assignments.

CLIENT scenario

Client J has been talking about the loss of her mother who died over a year ago. She is giving lots of details about her mother's last days and what happened during her mother's funeral.

Reflect on: Reflecting is the capacity to stand back to think again about something. It means going beyond the story or narrative, to think more deeply and to consider other meanings or hidden messages in the story. A theoretical concept may spring to mind when thinking about what the client has said. Reflection can also be part of the therapist's personal journey which has been stimulated by being in training and in therapy as well as through their clinical practice.

> THERAPIST journal extract
> *'J hasn't said how she felt at the funeral or anything about her relationship with her mother. I noticed she never said that her mother died. This makes me think this omission is important. I wonder what kind of attachment she had with her mother? She hasn't mentioned any other relatives at the funeral. What's going on in her relational world?'*

Hypothesis: This is your idea about a client which has not yet been proven or confirmed in the therapy.

> THERAPIST supervision notes after first session
> *'J has to show she coped with the funeral and is coping now – one year later. I suspect this comes from a background where she learned to put away her feelings and needs. She looks so together – is this her public face? She has just met me and is probably weighing me up as to whether I will be a reliable figure in her life. I wonder how reliable and available her mother was in her early life? I think she had an insecure attachment with her mother – probably an insecure, ambivalent one.'*

Explore: Explorers go into new territory to find something that has not been discovered, or has been previously discovered and then lost. Psychological exploration takes us into the unknown with our client and within ourselves, and in the therapeutic relationship.

> THERAPIST journal extract
> *'J has found it very difficult to talk about herself and her mother. So today she came back to talking about her mother's funeral and she repeated the story about the florist doing the wrong flowers for the wreath. I remarked that she felt let down by the florist. This word had an impact on her. She started to say that she felt let down by her Dad, who didn't come to the funeral because his*

new wife influenced him. J said she was annoyed with her stepmother for keeping her father away. This was the first indication of any anger and need I have seen in her over the weeks we have been working together. My comment had prompted a small step towards exploring J's feeling towards her parents.

It has also made me aware that this client's bereavement has encouraged me to talk to my therapist about my own relationship with my mother. My therapist has asked me to describe my relationship with my mother and I have said a few things that have surprised me. So a box is opening in me too. I am finding some memories of experiences with my mother, which is a bit disturbing.'

Discuss: This means giving the theoretical ideas and/or arguments about a specific topic. In an essay on bereavement, for example, the writing would show an understanding of theoretical ideas about loss and the grieving process, and critically discuss different or conflicting ideas, citing authors who have contrasting views. After presenting these arguments on the subject the therapist will conclude by outlining their learning from the subject and how the theory links to practice.

THERAPIST in essay (Introduction)
'This essay will focus on understanding theories around the grief process and what can happen as part of the grieving process. It will look at the long-established views of Kübler-Ross (1969) and compare with the work of Worden (1991) and Stroebe and Schut (1999). All these models will be referenced to clinical practice and evaluated in the context of my clinical practice in a placement.'

Demonstrate: This means show in practice how an idea or a skill has been applied to practice in a session. The therapist is no longer dealing with a theoretical abstraction but is actually applying knowledge or skill in their clinical work. Giving specific examples, if possible verbatim examples of the dialogue between therapist and client, is the best way to do this. If the therapist is recording their work with a client this affords many examples to choose from.

THERAPIST case study extract
'After several weeks' work with this client she came back to telling me again about her mother's funeral and I noticed that her voice was low and flat. She hadn't spoken about how she felt yet but I took a clue from her non-verbal signs and empathized with her by saying "I imagine it was a very difficult day for you as you felt no one was with you." She was silent for a few seconds, then slowly tears appeared. This suggests that I had timed my intervention appropriately in terms of what I thought she could begin to explore and that my response had caught a sense of her experience at this point. This was an important stage in our work and demonstrates the significance of empathic responsiveness.'

Evaluate: This invites the trainee to consider what they did well or well enough in a piece of work and what could have been improved or developed further. If the assignment is a theoretical one the therapist needs to critique theory to consider the assets of this theory and where it has limitations; citing published authors strengthens this argument. In clinical work it means the therapist can think about what helped or hindered the work.

> THERAPIST extract from case study evaluation
> *'I was aware that I was able to build a safe enough relationship with her by carefully listening to her story and giving her space to tell it. I did appropriately gauge the difference in her when she started to tell her story of the funeral again in week 12. My empathic response to her was key in allowing her to access her sadness about the death of her mother, which she had not allowed herself to experience before. It also enabled her to begin to talk about her relationship with her mother, which gave me the impression that it was a troubled one. What I could have done was to have been brave enough to let her know my impression of her as she talked about her mother. In addition, I also could have addressed the ending of the therapy more definitely – being more specific about when the sessions were ending, how she felt about the ending of the work and if she thought she needed more therapy. I need to think about why I did not give this the attention it deserved. Overall, in the 24-week therapeutic contract she had allowed herself to feel some buried emotions and had made an attachment to me. Therefore the losing of me at the end of the therapy was significant. This therapeutic process supported the client though her painful grief, and due to this experience I believe she will be able to speak to other people about her bereavement and make more meaningful connections with other people.'*

Analyse: This includes an evaluation of the work or some aspect of the work, but goes beyond an evaluation by acknowledging the significance of the issue being discussed. It means identifying the core or central issue and considering why this is important. An analysis can include what led up to the issue, how it was handled or not, and consider if something had gone wrong or was missed that in hindsight was important. Essentially, it means going to the heart of the matter.

> THERAPIST case study extract
> *'The death of the client's mother was a critical blow to my client's sense of worth. Throughout the work there was no sense that her mother had ever affirmed J. With the death of her mother there could be no repair of the relationship between them and this was deeply affecting the client. It evoked deep feelings of being unlovable in her and a core feeling of being lonely and unwanted. Ending the agency contract of 24 weeks probably felt like another abandonment for my client and I had not given this enough significance in discussing the impact of our therapeutic ending. So there was another lost opportunity for J to speak her feelings and thoughts about being abandoned.'*

Awareness and use of self: This is the sensitive and highly developed ability of the therapist to be able to read their own responses when sitting in the therapist's chair and then to discern how these responses might be relevant to the work with the client.

> THERAPIST journal extract
> *'Sitting with J today I was feeling quite bored. Same story again – what went wrong at the funeral – the flowers, the printing of the order of service. I felt like it didn't matter if I was there or not. Anyone could listen to this story. I felt quite redundant as her therapist. I was aware I was becoming angry as I listened to her. I need to take this to supervision to get some input on this.*

> THERAPIST journal extract
> *'Something happened today that's significant. Sitting with J I felt that sense of aloneness again. I looked at her and she looked so young, like a young girl, not a woman in her 30s. She had been talking about when her father left the family when she was a young teenager. As she was telling me about this I started to feel agitated or angry. I wasn't sure what that was about. Then she told me that after her father left the home her mother couldn't cope and would become out of control and violent towards her. When she said that, I felt so angry – where was any support for her? I looked at her but she was now crying. I had to decide if I could share what I was feeling so I found some courage and said, "I can see your distress as you tell me about this but I wonder if you might also feel angry?" She cried again and then through her tears said: "I wasn't allowed to be angry." This led to deeper exploration about how she felt about both of her parents.'*

There can be an overlap between many of the above key words; therefore use these definitions as aids to help you focus on your written assignments and on what you need to demonstrate in the work.

Written assignments: essays and case studies

It can feel quite daunting to sit down and put pen to paper or fingers to keyboard to write an assignment. I would offer one piece of advice: don't think about starting at the beginning of the essay or case study and then keep writing from this point. That is more the novelist's way of writing than writing for an academic purpose. However, preparation beforehand can break the psychological ice and get ideas flowing.

Self-reflection for preparation

Start with a brainstorm page where you let yourself freely write about the following:

- *What do I know about the topic/area of therapeutic interest or client (if writing a case study)?*

- *What theory and authors relate to this subject – or what important pieces of client history need to be noted?*
- *What examples do I have to show theory being put into practice?*
- *What have been my important learnings around this topic or client work and why?*

Brainstorming can help to free up thinking processes, and more importantly it shows the therapist that they are not an empty vessel looking at a blank page. It is a place to start. It can show where knowledge is a bit thin and the areas for further research before formally writing the assignment.

Having done enough study, the trainee needs now to put something together in writing. This is where a plan can help. Start by looking at the title of the assignment and its key words. Each assignment has an angle or focus, so try to get a good sense of what is required before starting to write. It's no good writing what comes into your head, even if it's brilliant, if the essay title is demanding a different focus. Training organizations for the most part set titles for essays rather than inviting the trainee to write about a subject that interests them. This is largely to do with assessment and moderation procedures. If all trainees are asked to write, for example, about the importance of allowing silence in practice, there is some expectation in the markers about what might be covered in the essay on this topic. This helps to encourage a level of standard academic knowledge on that subject.

Having gathered all the relevant information together, plan the assignment around three main sections. First, an introduction, which sets out what the essay is intended to cover. This is like setting out a stall. The reader gets an indication of what they can expect to read in the essay. Ironically, it may be better to write the introduction *after* the main section of the work because the trainee will know what they have actually written about!

The second section of the work is the longest. This is where you write about the question or theme which has been set in the assignment. This needs good planning in order to flow well. The trick is to organize any information, research and thoughts beforehand so that the writing comes out in an ordered fashion and connects together. Disjointed paragraphs that do not relate to one another do not make for a good read, nor do they convey that the trainee has put together ideas clearly in their head. As this section is the main body of the work, this will take time. If the assignment requires evidence of the application of theory to practice, give examples which demonstrate this.

Finally, write a conclusion to the work. This makes the reader clear about what ideas are important and where the trainee stands in relation to the theoretical ideas and arguments outlined in the essay. It can suggest further areas pertaining to the subject that could be explored or researched. Make sure there is a concluding sentence to the work so that the assignment is clearly completed. Also add a bibliography of the books used and reference any online sources that have been accessed.

Case studies are both a description and a reflective evaluation of the work with a client. A case study demonstrates how the therapist has worked with the client and understood their journey within the vehicle of the therapeutic relationship. These case studies show how the therapist makes links between the work in sessions and the theoretical concepts, and the theoretical model they have been trained in. In addition, the therapist needs to consider how clinical supervision has impacted the work with the client. In some ways, case studies are the best indication of how the therapist is relating theory to clinical practice.

When writing a case study, start with a section introducing your client anonymously to the reader (make up a pseudonym or use a number). Take note of any guidelines given by the training organization about the format of the case study and what must be included in it. In particular, notice if the guidelines stipulate a sequential case study (showing the progression of the work through the therapeutic sessions) which then highlights the main themes of the work and how the theoretical model was applied. Or, they may want a case study written in terms of the main themes of the work and your application of the model in the work.

In either case, in these formal pieces of written work tutors/markers are looking for:

- clarity of writing
- a clear understanding of the theoretical concepts relevant to the topic of the assignment or about the client
- a capacity to show thinking around the subject, not just a regurgitation of theory – so this includes an evaluation of the theory and an analysis of the relevance of the theory to practice.

Supervision presentations or studies

These studies require a specific focus on how supervision was used by the therapist and its impact on clinical work. Explain the reason for presenting the client in supervision (at that particular time) and what was discussed in supervision (points of view, ideas about what was needed in practice, any concerns raised in supervision such as ethical issues, safeguarding issues, issues of difference and diversity which needed attention, relational dynamics – conscious or unconscious – and what you learned from supervision). In conclusion, demonstrate through examples how the learning from supervision was taken back into the clinical work, and the impact of doing this. In some training assignments the case study and the supervision study are combined. Also see Chapter 4, 'Supervision'.

Presentations and research projects

At some point the trainee will be presenting, either by themselves or in a small group, a topic that is relevant to clinical work or on a specific theme or area of interest. It can be a delight or a frustration working with others to produce something for the group. Introspectively it invites reflection on collaboration with peers – how easy or not this is for the therapist. It may also evoke the old demons about judgement because the project is presented to the wider training group.

Some training programmes, usually at master's level or doctoral level, include research projects. An understanding of the methodology of research and the ability to use research methods (usually qualitative methods) in an actual piece of research relevant to the profession is part of the final assessment for the course. This research by clinicians in practice is becoming more important to the professional bodies, who want to encourage therapists to become involved in research as part of the ongoing development of the profession and as a way of providing evidence for the effectiveness of the work we do.

Specific challenges about assessment in therapeutic training

Writing assignments and completing all the academic components can feel like a challenge to trainees, when the course in itself is demanding enough. A colleague of mine used to say, 'Perfection is not needed but the assignment needs to be done.' All the assignments are connected to the therapist's development as a professional. If they can hold this in mind it may help the trainee to view the assignment as an investment in learning – not just an onerous task that has to be completed.

Another factor which makes assessment more complicated on a therapeutic training course is the position of the trainers. The tutors are qualified and experienced clinicians in their own right, but in their role of tutor have to assess a trainee's competency at different stages of the training programme. This can lead to tension between tutor and trainee. Sometimes trainees expect their tutors to respond more therapeutically to them rather than from their position as trainer. However, the tutor has to mark to the standard already set, which is not possible if they have to make allowances for any personal problems the trainee may be experiencing at the time. Trainees can find it difficult to fully appreciate that the tutor has to mark to a standard in order to ensure levels of competency and safety for the public and to ensure the integrity of the course's assessment procedures. Essentially, trainers hold the position of gatekeepers for the profession and have an ethical duty to the public to ensure that the trainees they qualify are personally robust, resilient, reflective and ethical practitioners.

Another factor is that professional competency and a person's development and readiness to practise are deeply intertwined. Tutors understand that training is disruptive and that trainees go through difficult and disturbing personal experiences when their inner psychological box is being stimulated and opened up. However, at some points in training ethical dilemmas may emerge about allowing a trainee to continue in training or to qualify. This is particularly difficult at or near the end of a training course if a trainee has completed all the academic requirements but the tutor team do not think they are ready to qualify. The training team need to be able to signal concerns to the trainee and to explain how to proceed and what is needed.

Completing: the view from both sides

It is gratifying for tutors to be able to endorse their students' competency as a counsellor or a psychotherapist and put them forward for qualification. For the trainee to complete a demanding professional course with all its different components is a huge achievement that needs acknowledgement and celebration. Satisfaction is felt on both sides.

7 The presence of the therapist

Focusing attention: physical presence and surroundings

Whilst listening to a client, both the physical and psychological aspects of the therapist's presence are engaged. These aspects impact on the client's experience of being in therapy, the therapeutic relationship and the space that is held between the two people in the room, thus creating the essential psychological container for the therapeutic work.

The therapist's physical presence is conveyed through their body posture, breathing pattern and facial expressions. The client, when they look at the therapist, takes in a sense of the therapist's embodied presence in the room. A focus in training can emphasize how the therapist sits in the chair. Sometimes trainees are specifically instructed how to sit when working. Apart from encouraging the trainee to be grounded and supported in the chair there is no need to be prescriptive about saying the therapist must not sit with crossed legs, although sitting with crossed legs and crossed arms is not advisable as this posture can look closed or defensive. (If the therapist realizes they are sitting like this it is worth them considering if this posture is giving a meaningful clue about what is going on in the dynamics of the relationship.) In practice it is more important for the therapist to be still, centred in their body and comfortable. Being appropriately still – but not rigid – is supported by regular and calm breathing. Developing a personal method of slowing down the breath and bringing attention to the moment is the starting place for being present in the room. Therapists need to be aware if their breathing pattern becomes agitated or irregular, so they can regulate it. Facial expressions are more difficult to recognize in ourselves. Generally, becoming aware of changes in our face, such as increased tenseness or being stuck in an immovable smile, is important. When we are comfortable in our chair, breathing slowly and regularly and having a steady but relaxed expression on our face, this creates a readiness to listen within the therapist and gives the message to the client that we are ready to listen to them. These points might seem small and indefinable but they are part of the basic conditions for doing the work, like a gardener getting their gloves and tools ready before starting work in the garden.

Another part of preparing is making the working space and atmosphere as tidy and calm as possible. When working in a clinical placement the therapist does not have a lot of influence over the physical environment but they can set up the room, arrange the furniture, open windows, place tissues strategically and gather administrative or research paperwork nearby, along with recording equipment if this is being used. Taking charge of these physical aspects can help the therapist feel they are making the room their own working space. All of these 'housekeeping' jobs need a bit of extra time so being early for the session is important. Running late or arriving just on time for sessions does not induce calmness in the therapist. There is no time to gather thoughts and prepare well for listening in a rushed state.

When starting clinical work a therapist might spend time considering what to wear for the work. There is often a clue in the agency itself: be aware of what the clinical manager wears. Sometimes there might be explicit statements about the agency's policy, such as a ban on wearing jeans. On the whole the therapist should keep a certain consistency and neutrality in their wardrobe and appearance so that these do not become the focus of the client's attention. If the therapist is spending a long time deciding what to wear it is worth considering what this anxiety or concern is really about. Clothes are containers for us but they are also part of our 'masks'. What is important is that the therapist conveys a sense of respect and professionalism by their physical appearance.

Physical presence online

There are practical considerations for online working spaces which will enhance your presence online:

* The background which will be seen on computer needs to be tidy and neutral.
* The lighting should be good enough so that you are clearly seen.
* The space needs to appear private and free from interruptions.
* The space needs to look the same for each session.

Focusing attention: psychological presence

This is easier to see and experience than to define. An observer in a skills session in the training organization can often see and sense the quality of a therapist's presence. A client, on the other hand, will have the direct experience of the therapist's presence and will feel if and when the therapist is with them. The essence of the therapist's psychological presence, although deeply individual, can also be developed over time as the therapist's competence and confidence grow. However, the key is the capacity to be present and available to the client in order to listen well.

Being psychologically ready is part of a complex and developmental journey that a therapist makes over their career. Here are the key aspects of what being ready to listen entails:

1 Physical presence – see above about settling body and breathing.
2 Separating the personal from the professional. The therapist needs to set aside their personal life and concerns for a time. This is a shift of focus from

the therapist's outside private life in order to be able to concentrate on the client. One way of thinking about this is to imagine putting all of your private life in a basket and putting the lid on the basket. Then the basket can be picked up and its contents reviewed at a later time when you are not working with your clients. This is quite a skill, but this ability increases with experience and self-knowledge.

3 Remembering purpose. A prime intention behind the therapy is to help the client understand themselves and in doing so find ways to alleviate their distress. Therefore, keep the focus on the client rather than your own performance. In the first instance, the quality of the therapist's listening and the steadiness of their presence will be the main contribution to the work.

4 Remembering support systems. A new trainee in a placement is being held within the support system of the organization. Additionally there is support in the training organization and supervision for the work. Remembering these different areas can help the new trainee feel held in a larger web of support and learning. There are also peers who will be going through similar experiences that can be respectfully shared.

5 Reaffirming the right to learn – acknowledging and accepting that this is the start of a new career and that there are many learning milestones ahead. These do not all need to be learned by tomorrow!

Self-reflection – preparation for listening

Here are two exercises you could use to help ground yourself before you work with a client.

Exercise 1. Before you meet your first client(s) imagine sitting in the room you will be working in. Take in the room – its size, its light, its colours, its space and its energy. Imagine seeing yourself sitting in the chair in a centred manner being prepared to listen. Have a sense that the room is also part of the container for the work.

When you have done this, reaffirm your sense of purpose for doing this work, while you imagine being in the therapy room. Consider how you feel and think now about starting your clinical practice.

Exercise 2. Here is an exercise with breathing and visualization for grounding. You need at least five minutes for this. There are several points in it where you can stop. Do as much as you want and what you are comfortable with. If at any point you feel uncomfortable, bring your attention back to how you are sitting on your chair and take soft, gentle breaths through your nose until you feel settled.

Find a quiet space for yourself and sit comfortably in this space. Take a minute to notice how you are breathing, without making any changes to your breathing pattern at this point. Then consciously allow yourself to breathe softly through your nose until you reach the top of your in-breath, then wait for a count of two. As you breathe out, imagine you are making a candle flicker gently with your out-breath. At the end of this out-breath let your body release any tension, e.g. move your shoulders, shake out your hands. You may want to repeat the breathing a couple of times.

If you want to proceed further here is a visualization. To do this it may be helpful to close your eyes or keep your eyes focused on a place in your room. Throughout this visualization allow time and space for your experience to be felt. (Later you might want to put the visualization on a recording for yourself if you find it useful.)

To start this visualization I invite you to imagine you are standing in front of a tree. It may be a tree you are familiar with or it may be a tree you see in your imagination – it doesn't matter. Allow yourself to really see this tree, noticing its different parts. As you look at the tree see where its roots are going into the ground and are anchored in the ground. Take your time to notice this. Then look at the trunk of the tree and see its shape and size. Again, don't rush. See the strength of the trunk and the flexible strength of its branches. Give yourself some time to see this tree. As you look at the tree you sense its grounded energy and vitality. You can imagine the energy as near to you as you wish. Stay with it for a while. Then notice how you are breathing and feeling. This is a good point to stop if you are not used to doing visualization. If you choose to stop, bring your awareness back to your body – notice your feet on the floor and your body on the chair, and breathe in a steady rhythm. Open your eyes gently to come back to your room.

Extension. To go a step further, imagine sitting in the therapy room with this symbolic tree near you – e.g. outside the window. Have a sense of its alive, responsive and grounded energy which can help support the sense of your presence in the room.

Consider for yourself if these exercises help to centre and settle you and if they would assist you in getting ready to work with a client.

The therapist's self-identity: connection and separateness

As well as attending to the client the therapist needs to notice what is happening within themselves whilst listening, and to be aware of their own sense of self in relation to the client. These self-reflective abilities come from being able to stay with your own self-identity. In essence, this requires a flexibility on the part of the therapist, who can resonate with and imagine what it must be like for the other in a situation but who does not become over-influenced by their client's experience.

It's akin to a professional gardener coming into a new garden at the request of its owner; the gardener can see, sense what is happening in the garden and with care respond to the garden owner and the situation without getting lost in the garden and giving up their own identity. Having a sense of their own self as a person in the first instance and then as a therapist allows the therapist/gardener to be separate but empathic and connected, whilst keeping to their role.

This helps the therapist to be able to think about the garden from a different viewpoint than that of the client/garden owner. The therapist may be pulled at times into the other's emotional world, and this needs to be privately acknowledged by the therapist and brought to supervision for discussion about what has happened in the session and in the relationship.

If the therapist is over-identified with the client's experience it will be difficult to keep therapeutic neutrality. Neutrality does not mean indifference. It means viewing and experiencing the client and their issues from a different perspective. This is essential if the therapist is to challenge the client to explore issues – what they have done to create the garden, how they deal with unwanted growth and how they want either to accept or change their garden over time.

Waiting patiently

The old proverb 'speech is silver and silence is golden' has many applications to training. It is easier to identify the components that make up 'silver' speech, as your trainers and supervisors will give you feedback on this. It is more challenging to deeply appreciate that being quiet, waiting with your client and being unhurried are fundamental elements of how to relate to them. New therapists can find this very difficult to do and it is a big developmental step for them. Being able to wait, to resist the temptation to intervene immediately, to allow the client to engage in their psychological processes in their time, to speak at a moderate pace – not rapid fire speech – and to quietly hold the space for the client is both respectful of the client's process and potentially facilitates their therapeutic journey.

The therapist's ability to wait with another without putting pressure on them to produce some finished product is a huge gift in our society, which tends to prize the instant answer and solution. However, waiting with a client does not always come easily.

> **Trainee voice**
>
> *'For me, being present involves coming to the shared space every week open to whatever it is a client may wish to talk about. Carrying the knowledge and understanding of what has been brought previously but "parking" it in the moment to be present, without any agenda.'*

The therapist and trust

All of the above require an ability to trust enough in life generally and in the therapeutic process specifically. Trusting is a complex process fundamental to human experience and embedded in experience throughout a person's life journey. No-one trusts deeply all the time. Trust is something that is built, waxes and wanes in relationships and is challenged by life experiences. The therapist needs to believe and trust that their presence in the room with the client is a fundamental building block of the therapeutic relationship and of the process of exploration and change. If the therapist does not have enough of this belief and trust, it's like the gardener who encourages their client to do something in the garden but doesn't really believe in the procedure or has not tried it for themselves.

One of the reasons why trainees are required to be in their own personal therapy, is to be on the receiving end of a respectful and trusting relationship. It is unreasonable in a therapist to expect a client to place trust in them as a listener and in themselves as a new explorer of the inner landscape if the therapist finds it difficult trusting life and others. Hence the therapist's own relationship to trust is crucial.

The therapist's relationship to authority

Whether the trainee likes it or not, at some stage they will be an authority figure or model for their client. How the therapist holds their own sense of authority is closely linked to their own sense of self as a unique and separate individual. Holding personal authority is not the same as being authoritarian – it is not about having power over another but about maintaining a sense of self which is distinct from the other. People who have been on the receiving end of the misuse of power and authority may find it very challenging to maintain a sense of their own self when working and may become over-identified with the client.

Concepts from the Transactional Analysis (TA) ego-state model (Berne 1961) are useful for understanding which part of the self becomes activated when working with clients. The basic ego-states are the Adult ego-state, the Child ego-state and the Parent ego-state. Stewart and Joines (2012: 4) define an ego-state as 'a set of related behaviours, thoughts and feelings. It is a way in which we manifest a part of our personality at a given time.' Understanding of ego-states has been expanded and refined to show much more complexity of the theory. For example, the Parent ego-state can operate as the 'Controlling Parent' or 'Nurturing Parent' and the Child ego-state can manifest as varieties of the 'Adapted Child' or 'Free Child' (Stewart and Joines 2012: 23). The Adult ego-state behaviour 'is a response to the here-and-now situation, using all the person's grown up resources' (Stewart and Joines 2012: 28).

If the therapist is psychologically based in the Adult ego-state they can be with and respond to the client appropriately. The client then has a good chance of sensing that there is a strong other in the room with them, which will facilitate their process. If the client thinks there is another 'child' with them it is unlikely to help the client explore certain issues which belong to their own story, or issues arising from the therapeutic relationship itself. For example, the angry young child part of the client cannot be angry towards the therapist if they feel the therapist is another vulnerable 'child' in the room. If the therapist responds from their own Adapted Child ego-state, it can mean there is a loss of neutrality and of the capacity to think about what is happening in more diverse and productive ways. Instead, here are two 'children' in the room. When this happens it is not something to be ignored, but needs to be thought about in supervision in order to find its meaning. The therapist needs to notice honestly if this is a persistent way that they relate to clients, and if so to consider what this indicates about their own personal processes.

Think again of the gardener who hears the frustrated garden owner wanting to pull up everything that is growing in the flowerbed. A too-ready agreement by the gardener to start pulling up everything in the flowerbed may result in losing the 'good' plants as well as the weeds. It may in the short term relieve the frustration and seem to be a course of action in moving forward, but is not to the ultimate benefit of the owner and their garden.

What is interesting is why the gardener has behaved in this way – losing their capacity to watch and wait, and thereby think and respond in a measured way. It may be that the gardener has become anxious – maybe they feel the weeds are growing out of control, or they may be resonating with the client's experiences of difficulties in the garden, which has impacted their capacity to stay separate at that point. There may be subtle and implicit dynamics influencing the therapist at this moment: for example, pressure of some kind which may be generated internally or by what is happening between client and therapist. Clients can have a bullying, pressurizing or seductive part of themselves which can cause the therapist to lose their own therapeutic position and capacity to think clearly and respond in a more robust way. For example, if a client is very positive about the therapy it may feel difficult to challenge the client if the therapist fears losing the client's approbation and that a challenge would cause a rupture to the relationship. If this happens over a prolonged period of time the therapist has lost their authority of the adult self, which is a detriment to the liveliness and effectiveness of the therapy itself.

The therapist is not the rescuer

Sometimes a therapist can be drawn into responses and actions that become an attempt to rescue their clients. The rescuer is one of the roles Karpman (1968) identified in the Drama Triangle – the others are the victim and the persecutor. However, the philosophy and practice embedded in counselling and psychotherapy's ethical position, theoretical models and formal training reinforce the stance that 'fixing' or 'rescuing' are not appropriate as they disempower the client. A new therapist, in particular, may be struggling to relinquish this role, often being unaware that they are actually doing it. This role and way of working often come from earlier experiences of being a young carer, either psychologically or physically, for a member of the family.

During training the role is usually revealed through skills work or when presenting clinical work in supervision and also in the training group dynamics. In skills work, rescuing tendencies become obvious when the therapist is trying to achieve an early or premature resolution to an issue the client is bringing, moving towards sowing seeds before all the soil has been turned over and prepared. The rescuing part of the therapist wants to keep something difficult away from the client – this could be a strong feeling or it could be the client acknowledging something difficult about themselves. Too readily trying to soothe the client hinders the client's opportunity to explore what is happening and how they are feeling. The gardener is saying it's the fault of the weeds that the garden is overrun, rather than reflecting with the owner on why there are so many weeds. The therapist may also try to do something for the client that the latter could do for themselves. This can come in the form of suggestions, usually loosely wrapped in question form. The therapist may also employ what I call 'pink bow' comments that attempt to make things better, thus minimizing or dismissing statements or feelings that the client has revealed (see Chapter 9). These 'pink bow' comments come from the therapist's unconscious agenda.

This rescuing of the client in a therapeutic context means the client does not 'grow up' psychologically, as they have not been through something in the presence of another who can hear them – warts and all – wait with them through thick and thin, and bear witness to their story, their process, their moments of insight, their times of despair, their times of deep acceptance of who they are as a human being walking through life in relation to others. Rescuing reinforces the client staying in a childlike, helpless or disempowered position and sense of self. And it rarely works!

Trainee voice – rescuing

'... it takes a while for trainees (definitely me) to see the different ways I rescue a client, so often rescue attempts are masked as interventions without the trainee actually realizing that's what they are doing. Self-awareness, feedback and spelling it out whenever I try to rescue, (and my) personal therapy – all together helped in my case.'

Self-reflection

- How much do I try to rescue others?
- Where does this come from in my own history?
- What might trigger the 'rescue' button in me whilst working with a client?

The therapist's own processes

Therapists find it challenging to stay present and be available to the client when their own personal issues are activated. A big culprit is the therapist's anxiety. Understanding the root of the therapist's anxiety is important. The outer reason is bound up with the fact that the therapist is on a training course and is being assessed and they want to succeed. However, their inner personal processes are also activated. This is most often generated by the question 'Am I good enough?' Underneath are usually deeper personal thoughts and feelings around being judged, feeling that being 'good enough' is not actually good enough, and what is really required is perfection – an insidious form of self-criticism.

All this is intensified if the therapist likes being in charge and is not comfortable with the unknown. Perhaps they have had roles in the family which put them in charge, or jobs in life which valued these qualities. Consequently, the therapist is uncomfortable with not knowing what the next thing will be in a session – what the client might say or do, and then what might happen between the client and therapist in the session. This discomfort plugs into issues about feeling out of control or of relinquishing control. If the therapist has experiences in their own history where not knowing the next step meant a threat or danger, there will be an understandable and usually unconscious fight to keep control in the session. This wresting back of control is most likely to come in the form of an intervention that breaks the silence – a question or a suggestion of some kind, or by trying to fix the client's difficulties. The therapist becomes like an impatient gardener taking charge by doing something in the garden that they think they have control over, and in doing so don't allow for the garden to develop in its own way and at its own pace.

The impact of being in training

One factor in creating this pressure is the assessment process itself. There is an inbuilt tension in the assessment process for trainees, in that the trainers need to hear the trainee's responses to a client, either in a class skills practice/goldfish bowl exercise or through a recording, which often means the trainee will preference what they *say to* the client rather than demonstrate how they *are with* a client. It is important for trainees to remember that trainers are also watching for the quality of the therapist's presence throughout the work and will notice when the trainee is doing too much or if they have become psychologically distracted (i.e. are not attending) in the session. When being observed by a trainer, the trainee's anxiety can cause them to do too much in the form of intervening instead of waiting for the client's process to emerge.

Another aspect of the training impacting on the session is the theory of the course coming into the session inappropriately. It is very valuable for the trainee to have a solid theoretical background, but sometimes these ideas are brought into the work when there is no need. The trainee linking in their mind what the client is saying to a theoretical idea is fine in itself. Where it does not serve the work is when the trainee feels compelled to share this idea with the client before the client has moved into this arena of thought for themselves, or when the therapist's intervention distracts the client from something else.

It's like the gardener thinking about the biochemical composition of the soil and what plants grow best in that type of soil – fine in itself to have technical ideas, but if the garden owner is wistfully remembering the roses from a childhood garden and is experiencing emotions as they remember their early experience, it is best to wait with them. The gardener might be correct in thinking roses will not do well in this garden, but suggesting this to the garden owner at that point preferences knowledge over staying with the experience of the client in the session – the feelings and meanings evoked by the memory of smelling the roses.

There may be a trainer's or supervisor's voice in your head. Again, these may provide valuable pointers for the work, but they can't be delivered in a session without an appropriate context and must come at the appropriate time. Otherwise it's like the gardener who hears their 'supervisor' say that all gardens need extra potash, and the gardener feels they have to impart this to the owner whether the owner is ready to hear this or not.

The therapist as a container for the work

In the 'therapeutic garden' the containment of the client is made up from the context of the therapy itself – the placement, its ethos and the contract between the placement and the client, which provides an essential foundation for the work. This is like the fence around the garden which encourages the therapeutic participants to work together in the private garden.

The therapist's presence becomes an essential element in the work that ensues. When the therapist is acting as a robust container for the work, the client will be able to impact the therapist emotionally, somatically, cognitively and imaginatively without diminishing or destroying the fabric of the container itself. I believe that the day when I can no longer be impacted by my clients is the day when I will need to give up sitting in the therapist's chair. What I mean by this is that if I, as a therapist, become impervious to my clients' feelings, their energetic sense of self in the room and the subtle energies that are conveyed between us, then I will no longer be able to work with a lively and responsive presence with them. I will also need to honestly acknowledge if endeavouring to be the container is too demanding of my own well-being, and if the answer is 'yes' to pay heed to it and make an ethical decision to stop working, either temporarily or in the long term.

The transpersonal container

Therapists who have been trained within a transpersonal discipline such as Psychosynthesis will also believe that the therapeutic work is held by a larger collective energy. When I was a very newly qualified therapist I had a client with a complex and challenging history who was very emotionally fragile. My capacity as a container was not as robust as it is now. My wonderful supervisor at the time – a transpersonal psychotherapist – invited me to do some imagery work about this client. She asked me to imagine seeing myself in my therapy room with the client and that a source of light was shining down on us and the light was holding both of us within its beam. This imagery helped me to feel that it wasn't just me that was holding the client – that there was something bigger than the two of us in this process. Similarly, in the garden the two participants – the owner and the gardener – can work collaboratively in a garden with clear boundaries but the light also affects what is happening.

Containing through listening, witnessing and holding

When the therapist listens in depth they hear, witness and are impacted by the strength of the client's feelings. They are also keeping in the mind themes and aspects of the client's narrative that may not be ripe for exploring. This involves a capacity to wait, not rush a client into exploration. Waiting can be difficult – a client might give a hint about something serious in their life but it is best to wait for them to return to this part of their story or theme. Essentially, the therapist needs to keep hold of ideas about the client, noticing what is alluded to in the story, and recognizing their own responses, which are stimulated or triggered by the material in the session.

The process of listening also means the therapist may be impacted by feelings from the client. Clients can unconsciously put into the therapist feelings that they are not ready to feel, acknowledge and explore. This is through the defence mechanism originally identified by Klein in 1946 (Klein 1988) and known in psychodynamic terms as projective identification (Maroda 2010; Howard 2010). Being in the presence of a client's intense feelings or being the recipient of the client's unconscious emotions can be very challenging and demanding for the therapist (see also Chapter 10 for further discussion on this).

A client I worked with had experienced the death of a parent through murder by their other parent. As they were telling me about what happened there was such a sense of shock, incomprehension and despair in the client. When they left the session, the weight of all these emotions was still energetically in the room and there was a residue left on me. I was able to bear it but I knew I was affected by what I heard and sat with. It would have been very negligent of me if I had not acknowledged to myself the level of impact on me of what had been transmitted to me. I was able to take care of myself after the session by 'purifying' myself psychologically. This restoration of my sense of self meant I was able to sit resiliently with the client in their next sessions and to continue working at depth with their painful feelings.

New therapists can take longer to cleanse themselves of deep and primitive emotion from the work and to recover before the next session. When we work with clients who have traumatic experiences, we are affected. In this sense the gardener needs to take care of themselves in order to be robust enough to weather the storms and vagaries of the seasons without collapsing or burning out.

The therapist's presence online

Online therapy does work *and* it is different.

The specific difference is the space in which the therapy is provided. Whilst working online, the therapist only sees the head and shoulders of the client and needs to be acutely aware of the client's tone of voice and facial expression, as other non-verbal clues are not visible. There is also a certain degree of intensity through this medium: the focus is predominantly on the client's face. The therapist's face and body generally remain far stiller than in the actual room, where gentle shifts of movement occur more readily. This means some natural movement in both parties – especially the therapist – can be inhibited online.

Both parties are sitting near their screens so the face-to-face distance on screen is much closer. This could be experienced as intrusive by either participant.

When working online there can be a tendency to intervene more or be directive at times, which does not happen as readily when working face to face. I think this is because there is a distance online that is not there when two people sit in a room together. This can be exacerbated by time lapses, frozen screens and glitches that sometimes occur online. Moments of thoughtful reverie can be lost whilst working online as the therapist can experience more pressure to prove that they are present and listening to their client all the time. The participants are not in the shared air space, which makes a difference.

Additionally, technical glitches that cause a client's or therapist's words to be missed or lost add some pressure to the communication. If this is a serious occurrence therapists may find themselves having to guess a few words or phrases that the client has said rather than asking the client to repeat themselves again. Clients may feel unheard by a therapist who has not fully heard their actual words and it is difficult for some clients to honestly share this as part of their experience with their therapist. These glitches can create a tension in one or both participants, as something in the flow of the communication is jarred or lost.

Care of self – care of presence – an ethical issue

The BACP Ethical Framework for the Counselling Professions (2018: point 91) states: 'We will take responsibility for our own well-being as essential to sustaining good practice with our clients by:

- taking precautions to protect our own physical safety
- monitoring and maintaining our own psychological and physical health.'

In addition, the Framework directs therapists to gain enough professional support and to keep a healthy work/personal life balance in order to remain robust to do the work.

Considering this in more detail, it is essential that the therapist feels well enough in themselves in order to be present and concentrate on the client. Protecting physical safety comes to the forefront in placement work when a therapist may be left alone in a building, especially in the evening, with little or no backup. Therapists can feel anxious if they are left to lock up premises after the last client has gone home. It can be supportive to have an agreement with another therapist who is also working late that you wait for each other in order to lock up the building.

To provide some added security some placements have an alarm button in the therapy room that the therapist can use to call for assistance if a client becomes physically threatening. The need to use this button is very rare in practice. Alternatively, placements suggest that the therapist sits near the door so that they have an easier route out of the therapy room if the client becomes aggressive and threatening or out of control. Again, this is a rare event in practice; nevertheless these measures offer a sense of security and reassurance for the therapist.

In terms of physical health, this is most often left to the discretion of the therapist to determine if they are well enough to do the work. Therapists work through colds and coughs – as do many professionals in other fields – as they do not want to cancel an appointment and let the client down. The therapist needs to weigh up the following if they are feeling under the weather:

- Can I still think about what I am doing and what I am saying?
- Do I feel well enough to give the appropriate and due attention to another?
- How will I be if I insist on struggling through the session(s)?
- What do I need to do to take care of myself at this point?

If a therapist is having recurring bouts of illness it is worth considering the psychological implications, e.g. stress levels or burnout. Taking care of ourselves also models a way of being which is particularly important for clients who are ruthless with themselves about having to carry on regardless. It's important to remember it's not the end of the world if a client's session has to be cancelled for a good reason. It will give the therapist and client a chance to talk about their relationship after the unscheduled break.

Taking psychological care of yourself is also important as more complex and demanding cases are coming into agencies and are being seen by trainees or newly qualified therapists. The critical question here is: do I have enough support – in particular supervision – in order to do the work without feeling overwhelmed? When the therapist feels unsupported, the quality of their presence is affected. It's like holding too heavy a load and being so concerned about dropping the load that this takes up all the attention and energy, rather than being able to think about the load and what it's made up of. For new trainees the load often feels very heavy. Hopefully with good support within the placement and supervision the load will feel manageable and anxiety about doing the work will lessen.

Self-reflection

Take some time to reflect on what you are holding:

- *How many very vulnerable clients are you holding?*
- *How many suicidal clients are you working with?*

- *How many clients mirror elements of your own story that you are still working through?*
- *How much strain and stress do you have in your life that puts additional demands on you at this point?*

Take some time to reflect on your support system:

- *Do you have enough supervision/professional support at this point?*
- *Do you have enough therapeutic support to help you contain your own psyche?*
- *What do you have to sustain and replenish yourself outside the therapy room?*

If you are psychologically under strain your capacity to be available is likely to be diminished or compromised in some way. It is important to be honest with yourself and then seek the appropriate help and support you need to work with more robustness. Caring for ourselves whilst working is an ethical duty, as it affects our ability to listen to our clients. Our ability to be present in the work is ethics in practice.

8 Mirrors

'Mirror, mirror, on the wall, who's the fairest of them all?'

Brothers Grimm, 1812

Maybe there is an element in all of us that's like the wicked queen in Snow White who wants to be acknowledged as the best by the mirror, which gives us back a reflection. Throughout the training period, and as we work professionally, we receive reflections of ourselves from various types of mirrors. Each mirror has a different facet of glass with which to see you and reflect back something about you. And you have your own mirror into your self – a hand-held mirror that takes courage and commitment to use. Like the wicked queen, we don't always get the response we hope for. If we are like Narcissus we stay stuck looking at our own reflection and think it is perfect, and then wither and die as a person and as a therapist. Sometimes we get a response that is more positive than what we see, as we look in the mirror. In any case, a training without mirrors and a therapist who doesn't look in the mirror and consider what is shown back to them is essentially locked into their own world.

The therapist as mirror

Professional training courses require trainees to have their own personal therapeutic counselling or psychotherapy. What is required varies from weekly or twice-weekly sessions over the period of training to courses which require a minimum number of sessions. So why do training courses require trainees to be in therapy? In one way it might seem best if the training organization simply left it up to the trainee whether to be in therapy or not. Research suggests that the motivation of the client is a key contributing factor in the usefulness of the therapy (Orlinsky et al. 1994, cited in Cooper 2008: 62), so if the trainee is there against their will and is just ticking boxes, what's the point? However, it may be useful for the trainee in this instance to consider a parallel scenario along the lines of 'why would I want to be a dentist if I had never sat in the dentist's chair?' I think it would be immensely difficult for someone to work as a therapist without experiencing what it is like to sit in the client's chair and engage with their own personal processes.

From a trainer's perspective they want the trainee to be in therapy for a number of reasons:

1 It is an opportunity for the trainee to have some private space away from the training room to think again about themselves in the presence of another. The Johari window technique (Luft and Ingham 1955) uses the concept of 'what is known to self and what is known to others'. Although this model was intended to be used primarily in groups, the basic principle can be applied to many aspects of personal development. Being in and engaging in personal therapy is an experience where there is the possibility of knowing yourself more and being known by another. This journey of self-discovery is of immense importance both personally and professionally. The more a trainee can work on their own personal material, the better chance they have of being a vehicle for another person to work on their story. A supervisor said to me when I was in training that you will only let the client go as far as you will go. I see trainees missing powerful emotional experiences in their clients – in particular the emotions of anger and vulnerability – because the trainee is still struggling to acknowledge these feelings within themselves.

2 The training process is stimulating but can also be disturbing. The training organization's primary focus is to teach the craft of therapy. It can be difficult for a trainee to reconcile the fact that they are being trained by therapists but that the classroom, although a reflective space, is not actually a therapy space. Having a personal therapist to talk to and explore what has been stirred up by the training is containing. In addition, starting clinical work can arouse a lot of anxiety. Clients can make a trainee feel uncomfortable, disturbed or inadequate. Although these responses can be discussed in supervision to determine if they have meaning in the context of the therapy, the more personal elements of these experiences are best brought to the private space for deeper exploration.

3 Given the demands of the training itself, the ongoing commitments from outside life and the psychological processes stimulated by training and working with clients, the therapy space and therapeutic relationship can offer support to the trainee who is seen and heard by their therapist.

4 The training therapist models ways of how to be and how to work. Regardless of their modality, the therapist shows through their practice what it means to be a professional. The trainee is learning from the example of their therapist. To this end some training organizations have a list of training therapists that the trainee must work with. The purpose of a specific list is that the training organization wants the therapist to have therapy in the modality that reflects the training model. This makes sense in many ways – it models the way of working and it's compatible with the philosophical underpinnings of the training model. Other training programmes leave the decision of who to have as a therapist entirely up to the trainee.

If the trainee has never been in personal therapy before embarking on training this can be daunting. There can be misconceptions that being in therapy only uncovers the painful and disturbed in you; that the mirror might only reflect back to you what is painful. However, the mirror may also show hidden positive attributes and potential that could be brought out and integrated into the trainee's life.

The personal journal: a self-reflective mirror

All training courses require trainees to continuously write and reflect on the impact of all aspects of the training on themselves, in a journal. However, courses vary in how they require this material to be presented formally. The Student Handbook for the course needs to state how the journal or extracts from it will be used to provide evidence of learning – for example, using reflections from the journal to apply theory to self.

The mirror of the experiential group

It is likely that in a large training group of over 15 the group will be divided into smaller experiential groups, although this is not always the case.

An experiential or personal development group is an open, non-structured, non-theoretical group; an open space made up of peers with a facilitator. Trainees can find this part of the training very challenging and often don't know what the purpose of the group is, or how best to share and respond in the group. It has many purposes, but a key element of this group is to encourage the trainee to explore themselves in relation to the other members of the group, and also to share how the training itself and being a member of a training group is impacting them. For some people being in a group is more challenging and increases anxiety more than the exploration in personal therapy, because there are more people looking at them and who could respond to them. On the other hand, some find it easier to hide or minimize themselves in a group in a way that is not so easy in the one-to-one therapy sessions.

Referring again to the Johari window (Luft and Ingham 1955), the group can provide an opportunity to give feedback to the trainee about how they present themselves in the group and how they relate to members of the group, which the trainee had no awareness of. For example, the trainee might feel very anxious about speaking out in the group and think they do not do this very well. However, feedback from the group conveys to the trainee that they come across as articulate, clear and open. If the trainee can accept this reflection from the mirror, it can begin to change their inner self-image. What the mirror provides is a glimpse of a different perspective. These perspectives may sometimes feel very challenging to the trainee if they unmask elements of the self which the trainee does not recognize and doesn't like.

Groups can be places of exploration for experimenting with communicating in different ways. This can include taking a risk in speaking honestly and directly in the moment. This can be a very big step for a trainee who has had experiences of being shut down when expressing their feelings. It is possible that being in the group and seeing peers share will implicitly or explicitly convey that it's acceptable to do this. In this way the group is a laboratory for experimenting with being and communicating with others that breaks habitual patterns.

Groups evoke feelings, thoughts and behaviours which originate from or remind the participant of being in other groups, in particular the family and school environments. Without being aware of it the trainee may be responding (directly or silently) to a peer or the facilitator in the way they responded to someone else in their life. This is what is known as the unconscious process of transference – see Chapter 10. For example, having a negative response to a peer who speaks a lot in the group needs to be considered in terms of where the reaction comes from. If there is the recognition that the response is an echo from the past which has come into the group, the trainee has a chance to do something differently. They could choose to take the opportunity to speak directly to the 'loud' one in the group and say how they feel about them. These choices to do and be different are challenges with potentially big rewards for psychological growth and development. Ingrained patterns of relating to others can begin to change. Doing this increases self-esteem, as a new facet of the self is starting to emerge. The experiential group is a place to start experimenting with this.

Groups can illuminate a pattern of social relating known as the Drama Triangle (Karpman 1968). Roles in this dynamic are unconsciously taken on by the participants, who can become the victim, the persecutor or the rescuer in the group and on behalf of the group. Most people do not realize that these roles are being activated and come into operation in the group. Comments from peers can increase the trainee's awareness of operating in one of these roles. For example, 'You jump in to find a solution the moment anyone expresses some problem' could help the trainee to recognize an unseen aspect of their personality. The comment could be useful in thinking about how the trainee responds as a therapist. Clarkson (1987) added the position of the bystander (or audience) in the group. The bystander needs to have their behaviours observed in particular when they stand by, when they freeze, when they don't say or do the thing that would be the most honest response from them. All of these behaviours provide information about inner processes which create interpersonal dynamics in the moment.

This unstructured group also evokes feelings, thoughts and reactions about the unknown and the unpredictable. Trainees who like to plan ahead, relish order and find security in knowing where the journey is going and the estimated time of arrival will find this aspect of training challenging. However, it may be that, in finding new experiences and ways of being in this group, the trainee begins to develop other tolerances within themselves. Being OK with the unknown in the experiential group will pay dividends in the therapy room, as the therapist will be more present, able to wait, and be comfortable enough with not knowing.

It takes courage to take the plunge to experiment with being and behaving differently in the experiential group. Sometimes the immediate effect is not quite what was hoped for. After reflecting, have courage to have another go – maybe some small adjustment is all that is needed to produce a different experience.

The large training group as mirror

The large training group consists of all the trainees and tutors in that training year who are on the same course (note that some organizations have more than one training course). The purpose of this group varies in different organizations. Usually course induction, making the working contract for the group, end-of-term or end-of-year reviews also take place within this forum. The main body of theoretical and skills training is usually done under the auspices of the large group.

Trainers decide if the large training group is closed or open over the whole period of the training. Generally the group is closed for the training year; then in subsequent years a trainee who has had a gap in their training may join the group. This is often the case when a trainee takes a year out for personal or financial reasons. There can be a feeling of loss when peers or tutors are no longer involved with the group. On the plus side, new people add to the dynamic and dynamism in different ways.

Whether at the start of training or when new trainees join, one of the key interactions that will emerge in the group is the dynamics of inclusion and exclusion. How the trainee includes or excludes themselves at times is a reflection of their own inner processes, especially about issues of safety in the group and belonging to the group. One way of looking at this is that the trainee has already made an investment in this group by committing time and money for the training place. The course trainers have also made an investment in each trainee by offering them a place on the course.

The large group is most often the place where the group processes of forming, storming, norming, performing (Tuckman 1965) and also adjourning (Tuckman and Jensen 1977) most visibly take place. Originally seen as a developmental model relating to a team, elements of this model play out and recycle throughout a training course.

Entwined with the above is the fundamental ingredient about how the training group develops trust: trust in itself as a group to work together and learn, trust in the training organization and trainers to organize and deliver the course that trainees have bought into, and trust in oneself as a trainee to make mistakes, learn the craft and learn about oneself. The process of building trust within the group is the foundation for solid learning. No trainee can train as a therapist and avoid the dynamics evoked by the training group, holding on to the erroneous view that they are on the training course to help clients and the group, and their experience in the group doesn't matter. If this is the trainee's mindset they will allow very little input from the 'mirrors' in the group, with the consequence that they are likely to remain voyeurs in the group rather than participants. Their own understanding of themselves will remain stagnant or at best limited.

Trainee voice – using the training group as a resource

'The main thing is that this group understands the trainee like no-one else. It can be an enormous source of support – emotional (because we touch on difficult material) and practical (whether it is a topic you want to discuss or just want a bit of a pointer for an upcoming assignment). Sharing experience and encouraging each other when starting a placement can encourage developing congruence.'

The mirror of being assessed

During training there is an intense mirror of assessment placed on the trainee. At the start of the journey this can feel in conflict with the basic therapeutic principles of acceptance and understanding. Points of formal assessment can feel like a personal judgement. In some sense it *is* a personal judgement – on the trainee's professional development and capacity – at a particular point in training.

All of this can create anxiety in the trainee. Not all of this anxiety is negative – it can show the desire to do well, and be a mark of eagerness to receive feedback in order to develop further. On the other hand, anxiety may also be part of the trainee's own habitual pattern around being judged. If the trainee has a particularly strong internal self-critic they might hear every piece of feedback as negative, and not what was positive or developmental in it. The trainee can be the most vehement critic of their own ability, but this may also be projected onto the trainer(s). If this persists without recognition, the trainee will have a stress-laden experience of training and will find learning in training difficult.

Self-reflection

- *How do you anticipate feedback?*
- *How do you generally respond to feedback, both in the immediate aftermath and later on?*
- *How self-critical are you? Where does this come from in your own personal story? How could this hinder how you use feedback whilst in training?*
- *What could help you to use feedback to enhance your work?*

For feedback to turn from evoking negative experiences into positive developmental mirrors there needs to be trust between the trainers and trainees. Transferential processes and other experiences of authority in the trainee's life can detrimentally inhibit this. Trainers for their part need to give clear, realistic, robust and encouraging feedback to their trainees, and to bring up serious concerns about them early rather than late whenever possible.

Your trainers and supervisors are in effect gatekeepers to the professional world. They have ethical responsibilities to ensure that trainees are robust enough to learn and to work in clinical practice at various points in the training journey.

Trainee voice

'Using feedback was made easier when I could understand it as part of a process of growth and development, rather than it being given to me harshly or punitively. At first, I felt that criticism was a rebuke to me for having had the nerve to think that I could be a counsellor at all. Being able to consider how the feedback could help me to refine my professional practice was empowering and supportive – I learned to feel that receiving critical feedback was part of respecting my role as counsellor, and helping me to fill it well.'

An overall view of the assessment mirrors

Using the mirrors well means that the reflection that is offered is given attention and considered. It does not always have to be swallowed completely, but the feedback does need to be thought about. If we are afraid to have a mirror and to look into it, the danger is of walking along restricting our view to our own perceptions and the elements on the road we already know about.

The mirrors offered to us throughout the training process are invaluable in helping us to develop professionally, which in turn helps us to be equipped to do the demanding work of listening in depth to another person. Mirrors continue to be part of our professional practice long after we have qualified, although their shape may change.

9 Working with feelings

One of the main shifts that trainees make in their work as they become more experienced is from being content-interested to process-orientated. What I mean by this, is that the trainee becomes aware of what is happening in the client and what is happening between the therapist and client, rather than primarily focusing on the client's narrative. Being able to work with the client's feelings is a fundamental skill for deeper process work.

We are embodied emotional beings who think and feel and live in our bodies. However, many clients have little knowledge of how they really feel or are unaware of their deeper, more complex emotional states. The therapeutic space provides an opportunity to delve beyond the 'I'm fine' response and to look more closely at the dynamic emotional inner world. The client is sitting with you because in some way something is not right at an emotional level, which is generating or contributing to their distress. Helping a client to become aware of their complex feelings states is central to the work.

Our feelings give us energy and vitality, colour our life, help us have contact with people and enhance our capacity to be creative and inventive. When our feelings are not serving us they can be overwhelming, consuming, keep us stuck in old patterns of relating and behaving, stop us thinking expansively, limit our capacity to make choices and engender an impulsiveness that does not serve us well.

Preclinical training in the classroom

Before working with clients in a clinical placement there will be skills training in the classroom with a tutor and peer observation. This is usually in the foundation year or a stand-alone Level 3 course. This skills training usually consists of practice exercises in a 'skills lab' where peers take rotating roles of therapist, client and observer. This year will begin to develop awareness of emotional vocabulary when listening to clients – the words, phrases and metaphors a client explicitly uses to convey a feeling state as well as their non-verbal communication. This seems simple at first but it involves high levels of attention towards the client. It is the start of the discipline for attentive listening and responding.

The therapist's relationship to their feelings

A capacity to work with and respect another person's feelings is reflective of how the therapist relates to their own emotional life. In training, tutors and supervisors observe closely the capacity of a trainee to work with a client's feelings. This is such an important part of the clinical work, and one that creates challenges for many new trainees at the start of training. Being in therapy is critical to being able to develop a capacity to work with a client's feelings. Everyone has feelings that they are more comfortable with – within their comfort zone. I have seen over the years trainees who are comfortable with working with vulnerability in a client but find a client's anger and aggression much more challenging. The reverse of this is also common. Another major challenge for new trainees is being able to wait for the client to reveal or indicate how they are feeling. Anxious trainees tend to use too many questions, which can distract the client rather than enhance the emotional exploration. Being able to wait is linked with the therapist's capacity to be present (see Chapter 7).

Self-reflection

Consider for yourself:

- *Which feelings within yourself do you know well?*
- *Which feelings do you accept within yourself?*
- *Which feelings do you find difficult to notice and accept within yourself?*
- *Which feelings do you find challenging when expressed by someone else?*
- *Which feeling can you listen to and allow in another but would find difficult to acknowledge in yourself?*

Then making a leap of the imagination:

- *Which feelings do you think you have excluded from the above reflections?*
- *What are you curious/surprised about in the above?*

Overall, from the above, what do you think you need to be mindful of at this stage of your training about working with another person's feelings?

The client's relationship to their feelings

In order to work with a client's feelings it is useful to develop observation skills around a client's emotional presentation. Whilst listening, begin by noticing how the client expresses emotion. Here are some key things to observe in a client:

- Does the client have a wide and varied emotional vocabulary or do they have a more limited one or hardly ever use words that signify an emotion?

- Do the feeling words the client uses fit with the tone of their voice and other non-verbal expression?
- Does the client convey their feeling through metaphor and imagery? Or do they allude to their possible feelings by talking about a film, a book or character in a book?
- Does the client use emotional language but not bring the energy of the feeling to the room? They may say they feel 'sad' but there is no sense of the feeling being energetically present in the room.
- Does the client think that their thoughts are the same as their feelings? An example of this would be in response to an open question 'How are you feeling?' when they say 'I think I am fine'.
- Can a client's awareness of their emotions help to facilitate change? A classic example would be 'I know it's not my fault but I feel it is my fault' – thus showing a lack of integration between the cognitive and the emotional parts of the self.

All of the above in a client will have been influenced by their psychological history, which has been shaped by how emotions were accepted or not in the client's family, their social and cultural background and in their education and other life experiences. Increasing our observation of how the client is expressing their feelings in the room assists the therapist in finding ways to respond to their clients' emotional exploration and expression.

Listening and responding to feelings

Think of a colander with large holes for draining vegetables. Then think of a sieve with a very fine mesh for sifting flour. The therapist collects and sifts the client's narrative whilst listening. The inner colander and sieve are filled with the verbal and non-verbal communication of the client's feelings and the impact of their psychological experience in the room. The therapist needs to internally become aware of what they have collected in their inner colander and sieve and consider its importance.

The client's words and story are the explicit level of communication. However, the therapist will also be receiving non-verbal communication from the client. This includes the tone of the client's voice, which could be soft, low, sharp, flat; and its rhythms, such as quick, fast, slow, slowing down, speeding up; the quality of the silence in the room (reflective, deepening, emotional, hostile, evasive); and the body responses and behaviours of the client. When I was in training, a senior psychotherapist and trainer revealed that he sometimes stopped listening to what the client was speaking about, which created gasps of horror in the group until he explained that he would listen to the client as if listening to music – so what was the quality or the tune of the music in the client's voice? Also revealing is the client's face, which will be giving clues – in particular their eyes, the muscles in the face, the tightness of the jaw, the client's gaze – which are all subtle indications of the client's inner states, especially when they change. All of these are indications of something happening within the client's inner emotional world.

Responding to a client

How the therapist responds to what they notice in the sieve is in effect part of the art of the profession. Trainers and supervisors will give guidelines as to what to look out for in the sieve or how to work with its contents, but there is no set formula for how to do this. With experience the therapist's sieves become finer and capture the more subtle emotional clues from the client's inner world.

Noticing all of the above is the first step. The trainee then needs to consider whether to respond or not. Sometimes it is enough to notice and keep the contents of the sieve in mind until there is an appropriate time to use them.

Explicit feelings

A good place to start is with the explicit feelings that the client is expressing. Reflecting back to the client their specific emotional words demonstrates first that the therapist has heard the client and second that you are comfortable with the client using this emotional language. A client I worked with was talking about her partner and how she was furious because the partner never helped with housework and preparation for visiting guests. I simply reflected the word 'furious' to her. If I had missed it or diminished it in some way, for example by substituting 'annoyed' or 'frustrated' for her word 'furious', I would have been giving her a message about what she was allowed to express in front of me – in this case, that being furious was not permitted in the therapy room. This kind of substitution is likely to come from the therapist's own uncomfortable reactions to that particular emotion. Sometimes new trainees get very anxious about reflecting 'big' emotional words even if the client has used the word, fearing this might upset the client. The client is more likely to be 'upset' if they haven't been heard (yet again!).

Restating an explicit feeling word back to the client also gives the client another chance to hear the feelings that they have named and to consider these emotions again. Words and key phrases can go down cracks in the client's narrative. A fellow trainee I knew when I was in training myself remarked that her therapist had said very little during one session but had just picked up and reflected back to her a feeling word which she had slipped out when she was talking but had given no attention to. Hearing this feeling word back from the therapist then enabled my peer to realize the word that had slipped out was full of meaning which she then began to explore. Its other effect on my peer was that she knew her therapist was with her and paying minute attention to her. The therapist's very fine sieve had sifted through layers of story and more surface emotion to collect the word with the greatest emotional meaning for my peer. The development of these very fine filters takes a long time. However, new trainees can begin to develop their own listening filters (Culley 1991) and in doing so help to create the foundation for establishing a safe and empathic therapeutic relationship which allows the work to begin.

Some signs that the client could explore further are that they have been able to hear their own words put back to them without dismissing, denying or ignoring them, and they have shown some capacity to go into a deeper process – i.e. feel more, think further or bring something up that has been hidden from view.

Implicit feelings – using open questions

Clients also give hints about their emotions when they allude to something or use metaphor to describe an experience, for example: 'It was like a tornado passing through.' The therapist's task is to help the client recognize the emotional and cognitive effect of being near or in the path of the tornado. The use of an open question could be useful in the above by asking 'How did you feel being near a tornado?'

Clients wrap up their emotional world in narrative; for example, the client has said they didn't like a remark a work colleague made to them, and then instead of telling you how they felt about the remark continues to give a lot of detail about the person who made the remark and its context. It is right and proper that this is listened to with respect, but the energy and psychological meaning of this incident is still not clear – either to the client or very likely to the therapist. In order to encourage the client to consider again the feeling aroused by this experience, make a gentle enquiry: 'How did the remark make you feel?' The client may or may not respond to this, which would be another clue in itself about the impact of the remark on the client and their readiness to feel the emotions wrapped up in this experience.

Implicit feelings – challenging discrepancy

The therapist can challenge a client's self view. A client with a negative view of themselves can often discount any positive attributes within themselves or in their experience, which can create a low mood in the client. Clients can then get stuck in habitual feelings and thoughts. A challenge made by the therapist aims to help the client see a wider perspective on themselves. One of the ways to do this is to make a discrepancy challenge (Culley 1991). For example, the client is saying that they don't fit in at the office but they have also told you that a colleague invited them out for coffee one morning. You could comment, 'So you are telling me about a friendly colleague at work.' Then observe the client's reaction to this – has it opened up a different view on themselves? If they discount it, then it is important to discuss with the client their difficulty or reluctance in shifting their viewpoint.

Implicit feelings – attunement

Attunement (Stern 1985) is the therapist's capacity to be with and respond non-verbally to the emotional tone and experience of the client. Attunement comes from the quality of attentive presence and non-verbal responsiveness that the therapist demonstrates towards their client. It is a tuning-in to the psychological energy of the client by the therapist in a non-verbal way. Stern (1985) describes this attunement as being 'cross modal', meaning the attunement occurs across the sensory modes.

For example, a client who has been bereaved and is recounting some part of their experience becomes silent and starts moving their head from side to side. The therapist, without thinking, is making a minimum response of 'oh' which is at the same speed and intensity as the client's movement of their head. The client's body movement is unconsciously matched by the rhythm of the therapist's non-verbal sound. These responses by the therapist cannot be engineered. They come from an organic, intuitive responsiveness from within the therapist and out of the therapist's committed and engaged attentive presence with the client. An observer in a skills practice session can see this quality of being in tune with the client more readily than the therapist observing themselves. In fact, if the therapist consciously observes themselves, they have probably come out of being in tune with the client. These experiences of attunement mean that the client begins to know or feel that the therapist is with them at that moment. All of this without words!

Implicit feelings – empathic responsiveness

In Harper Lee's novel *To Kill a Mockingbird* (1960), the central character Atticus Finch says to his daughter, 'you never really understand a person until you consider things from his point of view – until you climb into his skin and walk round in it'. Much has been written about the importance of empathy from across the therapeutic modalities, indicating and reiterating the fundamental importance of empathic attitudes and empathic communication in this work.

When we respond empathically to a client we are showing that we are seeing and understanding, as best we can, their experience in the moment, which is more than just the words they are using. It is like listening to a song – the words are important, but there is also the music, which gives a wider sense of the energy of the song and enhances the meaning of the words. Empathic responsiveness is picking up the essence of the client's experience from the client's perspective. It is a deeply intuitive ability of the therapist to do this. It is collecting together all the signs and information the client is giving – verbal and non-verbal – which gives the therapist clues about the client's inner experience beyond the story to how they are actually experiencing the event.

Conveying empathic understanding is best done tentatively. The therapist is conveying what they sense or imagine the client is feeling. We never know for sure, and even if we are correct it is up to the client to confirm that we have understood them in that moment. So the language of 'I sense you are feeling ...' or 'I imagine you are feeling ...' or 'I wonder if you are feeling ...' shows the therapist is trying to understand the client's experience without insisting that this is actually how they feel. It gives wriggle room for the therapist to consider again the client's experience and rephrase their response, or to wait for the client to speak for themselves.

Empathic responsiveness is essentially the therapist's capacity to make a shift from thinking about the client to a deeper, more intuitive sensing of the client in the moment and the ability to convey what they are picking up to the client. When empathic communication 'lands' with the client there is also an experience of what Rogers (1957) called 'psychological contact'.

For therapists who are naturally empathic it may be the case that they over-use empathic responsiveness. Watch the response of the client to these empathic offerings.

Implicit feelings – empathy towards interpretation

A client was telling me about all the notable people he admired in the world, both past and present. I somehow sensed this meant more than recounting a list of people he esteemed. In the session I remember strongly feeling that there was a message here and it made me really grapple with what he was trying to tell me. After some internal deliberation I said to my client that in telling me about these figures who he held in high esteem he was also thinking about his own value in life and that perhaps he didn't feel that important. My comment led to a fruitful exploration of how my client felt about himself. This intervention could be considered on the border between empathy and inter-pretation. The subject matter was there – important people in the world – but the deeper and hidden meaning for my client was wrapped up in it. He didn't realize that he was actually talking about himself and comparing himself unfavourably.

Implicit feelings – interpretation

Classical psychoanalysis would define an interpretation as 'The process of elu-cidating the meaning of something abstruse, obscure, etc.' (Rycroft 1995: 85). It is a response from the therapist that helps the client to see something that they are totally unaware of. In my own first experience of therapy (in a group) I was reeling off a list of reasons why I was feeling miserable in my life. Expecting some sympathetic response from the group, I was blown over when the group therapist interpreted my experience by saying that I didn't trust people. This was a total revelation to me. It never entered my head that I had trust issues. I thought of myself as sociable. I knew quite a few people and was on friendly terms with them. I was unaware that some of the issues that were making me miserable were coming from the fact that I didn't really trust others outside my close family. I was friendly with people but not close because I didn't trust enough. Until this interpretation was made I was unconscious that this was a hugely significant dynamic in my life. Having realized it and then started to make choices to reveal and give a bit more of myself when relating to others, my life began to change significantly. Therefore, an interpretation could be viewed as more of a high-risk challenging intervention. If the therapist gets the timing wrong – usually because there is not enough trust in the relationship or the client isn't open enough to really consider what has been said, or the interpretation itself isn't near the mark – then it could cause a breakdown in the therapeutic work. Sometimes the client makes an immediate repudiation of the interpretation but comes back later to talk about it further – this time interval varies.

Points to note about making an interpretation

1 Interpretations cannot be made to prove how clever the therapist is or that the therapist knows a lot of theory. The best interpretations I believe come from a deeply integrated and intuitive place within the therapist and are made as a thought offered to the person sitting in front of them.

2 Some training courses will not encourage the use of interpretation by the therapist as their theoretical model would view this as the therapist being too directive, and that any deep insight best comes from the client themselves. I agree with this rationale for working, and I also believe that an interpretation could be crucially important. It is significant if, through the work, the client can come to see something about themselves without a therapeutic interpretation. However, I am immensely grateful that a therapist saw something in me that I was blind to and she appropriately offered me a different view on myself. Whether to make an interpretation to a client is a moot point in theory and practice between theoretical modalities. The trainee will need to be very clear about whether their training modality works with interpretation and unconscious processes in this way.

3 From the personal perspective of the therapist's own therapy, if the training therapist does not use interpretations, there will be no experience of receiving and responding to an interpretation. It would therefore be inappropriate to use this way of working with a client.

Although various skills for working with feelings in clients have been defined separately above, in practice therapists work with a variety of responses depending on the focus of their training and their own confidence at the time, and in relation to the client who sits with them.

Working with conflicted feelings and competing parts of the self

Sometimes a client doesn't have a single main feeling state. Instead, there may be internal conflict between different parts of the client. For example, a client tells you about their dilemma over whether to end the relationship with their partner. The client has been offered a dream job in another part of the country but their partner will not make the move. On one level this is about the different needs of the two people in the relationship, but the focus will be to help the client understand the struggle within themselves caused by this decision. This inner struggle can be understood in the Transactional Analysis (TA) model (Berne 1961; Stewart and Joines 2012) as tensions between the different ego-states of the client or what are known as subpersonalities in Psychosynthesis (Assagioli 1965).

In terms of the above example, the competent, professional part of the client dominated by reasoning about developing their career is set to move, but the more vulnerable and needy part which is afraid of being alone may be willing to stay put. The therapist is holding in mind and working with these competing parts of the client's self to help the client understand where their feelings come from, and which have the most weight for them at this time.

In general, some of the common themes around a client's conflicts centre on:

- the need to keep safe and the desire to feel free to be or do something else
- the impulse to speak out and express oneself and the habit of repressing their own voice
- the risk of reaching out or doing something new in a relationship or situation and the familiar practice of not trusting and remaining in known relational states and behaviours.

These conflicts can create huge emotional battles within the client. If they are not resolved or softened in some way the client will remain torn and unable to move on. The therapist's job is to help the client to become aware of their inner conflicts, with their different emotional and cognitive pulls; then to explore what is most important for the client at this time, taking into consideration their head and heart responses.

Tension between waiting and naming

There can be a tension between giving the client time to come to know how they are feeling at a deeper level and the therapist empathically sensing what the client might be feeling and naming the possible feelings. Part of this tension comes from the way theoretical modalities put different emphasis on to what extent the therapist names the client's feeling – either in an empathic way or through an interpretation – and at what point in the work. Into this mix is also added the engagement and reflexivity of the client. If the client can share their own feelings, then the therapist can hold back, as the client is doing the work. Sometimes, however, clients become blind to their own feeling states so the therapist then makes a decision about how to respond.

In the example above, the client is discussing their life situation after a relationship breakup. The client is reporting how they are coping and what they are doing practically to move on. All of this is fine in itself, but the therapist senses that underneath the brave and coping face the client still has a lot of feelings about the end of their relationship. Here are some possible ways of working at this juncture.

First, the therapist could wait and let the client come to realize that they still have emotional responses associated with the breakup. In open-ended work this seems easier to do than in time-limited work. However, think about waiting – maybe the client only needs a small amount of time to come to their own realization. If the therapist is feeling under time pressure this could be transmitted to the client to acknowledge their feelings before they are ready.

The therapist could take a more tentative empathic approach by offering their sense that the client still has a lot of emotions around all these significant changes, thus inviting the client to contemplate their underlying experience.

Another approach is that the therapist could be more interpretative and offer the idea that the client may be feeling betrayed by the breakup and the broken promise of the relationship. This would be the therapist going beneath the explicit dialogue to offer their own sense of what the client is feeling at a deeper level – a level that has not been brought explicitly to the room.

As a trainee in the first place, it is best to be guided by the theory and practice of the training model and supervision input.

Pressing the pause to reflect button

With some clients who are caught up in their own narrative or who are pursuing their narrative unconsciously to keep away from a deeper reflection, the therapist may need to deliberately slow them down. I think of this like using the pause button. I say to clients, 'Let's press the pause button for a moment' and if I think they have said something significant and skipped over it I may add 'because you have just said something important which deserves attention'. The intention is to invite the client to consider what they have said and to give attention to what actually had significance or emotional impact. If the therapist has to do this repeatedly, then they will need to discuss this with the client. Inviting this discussion could be experienced as a high-level challenge from the therapist, so it needs to be used with caution and within the context of how the relationship has developed.

Trainee voice – difficulties of working with a client's feelings

In class discussion the following comments were made about some of the difficulties in working with feelings:

- *Defences of the client – either client resistance or self-protection.*
- *What to do when the client refutes your empathic suggestion?*
- *Dissociation from feelings.*
- *Client being stuck in cognitive mode.*
- *Client being stuck in narrative mode.*
- *Reading body language for clues to underlying feeling can be made harder by using Zoom.*
- *Timing – how to go at your client's pace, knowing when to make an intervention about feelings so as not to push the client before they feel safe enough.*
- *Time-limited: challenge of working at the client's pace within this contract.*
- *Client missing sessions – stalling the progress of the work.*

What helps to overcome these difficulties:

- *Allow space, go at the client's pace.*
- *Communicate emotional warmth and safety that encourages your client to feel comfortable going deeper; be a safe container, regulator.*

- *Use relational immediacy when appropriate.*
- *Use judgement when challenging.*
- *Really focus on picking up 'heat' words (words with energy).*
- *Use the client's body awareness – where in the body might they be feeling something?*
- *Grounding myself – breathing, pausing.*
- *Using supervision.*

Why is it important for a client to experience their feelings in the room?

For many clients the past history of their own emotional expression is a limited or troubled one. Very few families allow a broad spectrum of emotions to be expressed within the family context. Consequently, emotions get suppressed or even repressed in the early life of the client. At some level, therefore, the client comes to experience their feelings as not valid, or not as valid as someone else's, not real or not 'correct', or 'bad' in some way. Most of the time the client doesn't recognize that this is what they are doing to themselves. When the therapeutic work begins to give them the experience of being heard, they may find a place and a space to bring out what has been locked up or covered.

It is a crucial shift from *talking about* feelings to actually *feeling them* in the room. It is significant when the client makes this transition – to feel in the presence of another person who is not judging or denying their emotional experience. This can help the client to be less overwhelmed by having and expressing their feelings. They begin to learn that the therapist is not diminished, destabilized or destroyed by hearing feelings and having them expressed energetically in the room. This potentially allows the client to experience (possibly for the first time) that what they feel may not be so disturbing or dangerous as they thought.

If the client has a lot of inner shame – often unknown (Mollon 2002) – revealing feelings can feel very exposing. However, if the therapeutic alliance is strong enough for the client to express and release their feelings this can be hugely cathartic. Something is now in the open, no longer secretly held inside the client but shared in the presence of another non-judgemental human being.

In addition to this validating and witnessing by the therapist, the client is also being contained by the therapeutic presence. Their feelings are not going into a void, as the therapist is acting as a psychobiological regulator of their feeling states. The work of psychoanalyst and neuroscientist Allan N. Schore has broadened our understanding of how we impact on each other. The therapist is actively containing the client's feelings by their robust and empathic presence. He refers to a piece of therapeutic work with the traumatized mother of a young child and its effect on the mother: 'The burgeoning therapeutic alliance in turn allows the clinician to act as a psychobiological regulator of the mother's dysregulating affective arousal …' (Schore 2012: 414). The therapist's presence and way of being with the client helped to calm and settle down the client's emotions.

Emotional release – end of session and in the next session

If there has been a big emotional release of feeling it is important that the therapist acknowledges this, and they may need to check out how grounded the client is at the end of the session. Are they safe enough to go home? Acknowledging the enormity of what the client has gone through emotionally can feel very supportive to the client and be containing for them. This is also a potentially reparative experience for the client, in that the therapist has seen the released and often distressing emotion and is concerned about how the client takes care of themselves. The therapist may not need to do anything practically but they do need to acknowledge the client's process.

It is also important to notice how the client is in the next session. There may be a closing down as a result of the previous week's work. The client might need to go to a quieter emotional space as a way of regulating themselves. If this persists and there is a more long-lasting steering away from feelings, there needs to be a discussion around what happened in the session and how it has left the client feeling about themselves and what they revealed. Feelings of shame might have emerged after the session because the client felt they revealed too much. Or perhaps the session left the client too disturbed for a long period. If the work on deep emotions is to continue fruitfully there needs to be further exploration about the effects of the session. Find a way to respectfully and empathically talk to the client about what has happened and invite their response about it.

Examples of when working with feelings needs modifying

Clients who do not know what a feeling is or have a very limited sense of a feeling world will not understand enquiries about their feelings or be able to take on board empathic responses about their feelings. For example, a client I had who was a successful businessman had been encouraged to go to therapy by his wife. He didn't quite know why he was with me and he was certainly perplexed by his wife's emotional demands for more psychological closeness. In his view of himself, he was a faithful, intelligent and hard-working husband. I could see that he was all of these things, so from the start we had the underlying difficulty about his motivation to be in therapy but nevertheless he showed up for all of his sessions. In an early session he spoke of a business-related difficulty he was having which involved a new business partner. I intended to be empathic and said that it must be challenging and stressful for him to have a new business venture and a new colleague. He totally dismissed it and went into a problem-solving mode in front of me. I learned that this man did not examine his own feelings, and if our working alliance was to stand any chance of being sustained I would have to find another way to connect with him. I would have to go through what Ware (1983) calls a 'door to contact' in order to communicate with him. Ware identifies that each person has a contact door – thinking, feeling and behaviour. The therapist needs to be aware which is the client's 'open door', then use this as a point of contact and communication before moving to their 'target door' – 'in counselling or therapy, this is often the area in which most of the overt "work" gets done' (Stewart and Joines 2012: 178). This client's door was the thinking mode. Clients predominantly in thinking mode do not understand the question 'How do you feel right now?' It's not how they operate in the world, so cognitive reflections or a form of cognitive empathy, e.g. 'perhaps you see it like ...', leaving out feeling words, are more useful to start with. Being more cognitively empathic with him and helping to build some awareness of his body states, e.g. where he had a physical pain or tension, was a better route to helping him gain a fuller understanding of his experiences.

Another client, who had a long history of chronic conditions of neglect (Fisher 2017) and abuse, was difficult to make contact with. I found myself in one session trying to reach out to her by responding as empathically as I could. It was having no visible effect on her so I had to reflect on what was happening between us. I became aware that I was overfeeding her with my empathic responses. I realized that she wasn't used to being empathically responded to. She needed my responses to be offerings of 'baby rice' not 'fillet steak' empathy. She couldn't digest or use what I was trying to offer her. All of this made sense in the context of her early family experiences, where she received little attention and felt unsafe. Consequently, she found it very difficult to trust people. This unconscious way of being with others in the world came into the therapy but I had not considered it until I saw that my attempts at making contact with her were falling flat.

It was a good learning experience for me as a new therapist to acknowledge that all the work ultimately sits within the therapeutic relationship itself. Building a working relationship with trust is a necessary prerequisite for this level of work with a client's emotions. However, if the trust is not there, then the therapist needs to open up a discussion with their client about the therapeutic relationship itself (see Chapter 10) or the work will not be able to move forward.

Containing feelings

Up to this point the emphasis of the chapter has been on facilitating the expression of explicit feelings or buried ones, and this is indeed a very large portion of the work in therapy. However, there are times when working with feelings needs to be done with caution, either not at that time or with the intention of helping the client bring down their emotional intensity by helping them regulate their own emotional arousal. Clients have a 'window of tolerance' (Siegel 1999, 2010) for how much emotional arousal they can bear at a given point.

There are several reasons why emotional regulation is important. Some clients have intense emotional energy and rapidly changing feelings. The difficulty with this is that the client can be overwhelmed by what they are feeling, to the detriment of being able to think about themselves or hear any response from their therapist. They can become consumed in the sense that their feeling state is their total reality and always will be! If this is the case, they may become locked into long periods of emotional storms – some greater, some lesser. Such prolonged times of intense emotion are exhausting, can be physically debilitating, and can lead to decisions made out of reactive emotional responses rather than a measured response. They impact everyday functioning and relationships in life.

In the therapy room the therapist will be helping the client to contain their feelings so that they are not so overwhelming. To facilitate this, use what I call the 'making small' emotional approach. It starts with the therapist's ability to avoid getting caught up in the maelstrom of emotion but to maintain a calm and steady presence in the room. Acknowledging the client's explicit feelings and empathizing with their emotional distress reaffirms that the therapist has heard them. This can be hugely significant in helping to contain a client's emotions, especially if those emotions are triggered by experiences of being dismissed or ignored. For example, saying 'I can see you are very angry now' bears witness to the client's experience and often results in the client calming down – although not always immediately, so stay with it! I think of this as trying to turn down the heat under the pot for now. It's not denying that the pot is full and it's not turning off the pot for ever. It is intended to keep the pot from spilling over at this point. When the temperature of the pot falls there will be an opportunity for exploration and understanding of what was triggered. Clients who are in a highly emotional state don't think well and don't see the bigger picture of their life and its unfolding journey. The therapist's ability to help contain their emotions is very significant.

There is a very useful technique called disidentification (Assagioli 1965) that comes from Psychosynthesis. Without going into all of the technique, it helps the client to get a sense that they have feelings, but that feelings change and who they are as a person is more than just the emotional state they are experiencing at the time. A phrase such as 'You have feelings but are more than your feelings', or as I said to a client, 'You have anxiety but are more than your anxiety', can give a space from the overwhelming emotion of the moment. It gives the client a sense of a larger identity rather than the intense feeling they are in. Using a disidentification phrase as above is more directive on the therapist's behalf and needs to be considered in the session and afterwards.

There may be times when a client is in a highly agitated state when specific techniques such as mindfulness may be very helpful to them; or the client can be helped to slow down by learning to regulate their breathing. The therapist would need to have had some training for these techniques to ensure competency. I am just signposting them here.

Clients who have trauma in their background, either complex trauma from ongoing abuse and neglect (Herman 2001) or a more specific trauma, may become triggered and show signs of dissociating. In these instances the therapist needs to be as containing as possible, facilitating the client to become grounded in the room again – back to the now. If it becomes known to you over the course of the sessions that your client has a severe trauma in their background it is crucial that you work slowly and under close supervision. This may be a point where you do some specialist reading or training. It might mean that as a new trainee your skill set and level of training do not match the level of competence and experience that the client needs.

Reasons why working with feelings can become interrupted

- Distraction. This is when the therapist is distracted by the work. The most likely cause of this is that the therapist's own material is being activated or the therapist is uncomfortable with the feelings being expressed in the room. This makes it incredibly hard for them to remain focused on the client.

- Control. There are several ways in which control dynamics affect how the therapist works. If the therapist prizes information about parts of the story or people in the story so that the feelings are missed or dismissed, this shifts the focus of both client and therapist. It's important for the therapist to reflect whether they want to know this detail out of curiosity or because it gives them a sense of control. Another sign of this is the overuse of questions by a therapist. In new trainees the very natural feeling of being anxious, because this is new clinical experience, can cause them to use a barrage of questions in the session. By doing this the new trainee who feels out of their depth tries to wrest back control by using directive questions. Even the overuse of open questions is directive.

- 'Pink bow' responses. These happen when the therapist wraps up what the client has been talking about in an overly positive way. This often comes towards the end of the session as a kind of tidying up of the client's emotions. Therapists who do this are unconsciously responding out of something in their own process, e.g. a dislike of a messy ending, a fear of leaving the client in a messy state or a fear that they are a 'bad' therapist who lets the client leave with difficult emotions. The 'pink bow' diminishes the reality of the client's experience.

Working with feelings online

Some of the challenges of working with feelings online are:

- Technical glitches, e.g. delayed speech of the participant(s), frozen screens and loss of connection, may occur at important points in the session and disrupt the client's process. This poses a challenge of helping the client to return, as much as possible, to the feeling state they were experiencing before the glitch.

- The client is only seen from the shoulders upwards so you don't see their whole body – no twitching or kicking feet will be visible!

- It can be more difficult to pick up subtle energies emanating from the client.

- You are not near the client and your capacity as a regulating other (Stern 1985) may be reduced.

- It may seem harder to allow silence and to wait with the client in online work.

The capacity to work with feelings and its impact on the trainee

1 This is an area that will be keenly observed and assessed by trainers and supervisors so it is an essential aspect of the therapist's professional growth and skills development.

2 Working with a client's emotion is also very demanding on the therapist, especially when working with clients in high levels of distress or hopeless-ness and when they are presenting with suicidal ideation.

3 Working with a client who is negative or aggressive can feel like a blow. Having an understanding of the possible dynamic in the relationship can help the trainee to stay as stable and calm as possible in their own sense of self.

Overall, working with clients' feelings is a rich and rewarding experience. Being a witness to a client getting in touch with long buried emotions, working through them and finding a new sense of self and freedom from this process is gratifying.

10 Working with the therapeutic relationship

Interpersonal dynamics

When it comes down to it, the therapeutic relationship is about two people sitting in a closed and private room for the purpose of helping one of them, the client, to explore themselves and how they live their life and relationships in order to live a more enhanced life – whatever that means for the client. Whilst the focus is on the client and their needs, being in a relationship with another person has an impact on both people. How the two participants work together is an important factor in the outcome of the work. 'The quality of the therapeutic relationship is closely associated with therapeutic outcomes, across both relationally orientated and non relationally orientated therapies' (Cooper 2008: 125).

Clarkson (1993: 39) acknowledged that 'five forms of relationship are intentionally or unintentionally present in most approaches to psychotherapy', although therapeutic modalities may not explicitly use all of them within their model and theory of practice. These relationships are: the working alliance, the transferential/countertransferential relationship, the reparative/developmentally needed relationship, the I–You relationship and the transpersonal relationship. Since this meta model was proposed by Clarkson, most modalities would now include an understanding that the relationship also has social and cultural elements. That essentially the therapeutic relationship is complex and fluid. That the different relational aspects can be mutually influencing and reinforcing. Whether it is explicit or not, there is always a relational dynamic between the therapist and their client which is present and changing throughout the work.

It is a big developmental step and challenge for trainees, in terms of their skill set and confidence, to begin to talk to a client about what is happening in the dynamics of the therapeutic relationship – what you could call 'us' talk or 'you and I' talk. Culley (1991: 87) writes: 'Immediacy can be used to focus on the relationship between counsellor and client.' Beginning to make use of this relational immediacy can create anxiety in the therapist, as the therapy is not simply about the client any more because you, the therapist, are now brought onto the stage and under the spotlight with the client. What you say to your client on this relational stage will be like a careful and measured response which invites the client to make another response to you. At certain times in the therapeutic process this form of dialogic process needs to take place if the therapeutic work is to remain effective and fruitful.

Self-reflection

*In terms of where you are in your training and clinical practice **right now**, take some time to consider these questions:*

- *How confident do you feel to engage in a conversation with your client(s) about what is happening between you?*
- *What helps you to do this? Is it something to do with you or is it something to do with the client?*
- *What reservations do you have about engaging in 'you and I' talk at this point?*

Thinking about your own experiences in therapy, consider:

- *How does your own therapist talk with you about what is happening between you?*
- *How do you feel about these exchanges?*
- *What could you learn from them?*
- *Does your experience with your therapist influence whether you are confident in working relationally?*

All is new – the fear of exposure

It is easy to forget that some clients are very fearful about what may happen when they come to therapy. It is a huge step to make a call or send an email asking for therapeutic help. On the other side, a new therapist in their first placement may also be wrestling with their own fears about embarking on clinical practice. So how are two anxious people to relate to each other in the room? Both participants may feel very exposed, for different reasons. It does fall within the remit of the therapist to contain their own anxiety as much as possible, in order to provide a calm therapeutic environment for the client. Taking some time to settle down, finding a sense of your own presence and believing in your own readiness to start working as a therapist can be beneficial. The ability and confidence to work in clinical practice does develop once the trainee therapist has some experience under their belt, so take heart!

For the client, the fear of revealing themselves may continue for a longer time. It is possible that the client revealed salient aspects of their life when they met the assessor for the first time. If the client revealed their big 'secrets' to the assessor it may be that they have become more psychologically defensive by the time they meet their therapist, especially if there has been a long waiting period between assessment and beginning therapy. Facing a new person again and revealing their struggles may feel very uncomfortable for the client. Talking about this situation is important. You could say, 'It's been a long time since you met with the assessor and now you are meeting a new person to tell your story to. I imagine it's difficult to have to start again.' This time it's not a one-off meeting but the start of a new relationship. If you have a sense that the client may be having reservations about you, finding a way to open an exploratory dialogue can be very useful. 'I wonder if there is something about me that may be causing you some concern in speaking?' Being as explicit as this is a bold move by a new trainee so you may not feel confident enough to do it with your first or early clients. Too much of the spotlight may be on you at this point rather than just being on the client.

By being in the room with you, the client is admitting that there is something they are finding troubling which they cannot remedy themselves (Howard 2010). This may be very difficult for the client to accept. Although the client has sought help it doesn't automatically follow that they are ready to share more and immerse themselves in deeper psychological processes. The client also has to get the measure of you as their therapist and themselves as a person engaging in an inner journey. It takes time before they can allow themselves to be in touch with forgotten experiences or hidden feelings within themselves. In addition, if this is the client's first experience of psychological therapy they will have no map of what to expect or how they can use therapy in their own best interests.

Engaging in therapy – trust, vulnerability and power

There is no simple formula for knowing what will work in the therapeutic relationship. However, no real exploration will occur unless there is a feeling of safety in the relationship. Building a robust enough relationship takes time and commitment on both sides. The relationship is by its nature an arena where issues of trust, vulnerability and power (Proctor 2017) and privilege (Turner 2021) will be present either overtly or subtly. These issues will be influencing the dynamic between the therapist and the client all the time, but especially at the start.

When the client seeks therapeutic help it implies that the client comes to the agency having some sense of helplessness and possibly vulnerability about a problem or issue in their life. This has two implications: first, has the client some willingness (consciously or unconsciously) to bring their vulnerability to the room? Second, can they begin to trust the therapist as a person who can help them reveal and explore their issues? The client will be weighing up their experience from the start.

One factor in the question of trust in the therapist centres on how the client perceives the position and power of the therapist. For some clients there could be the mistaken idea that the therapist may be able to fix them or take away their pain, so the client lays everything before the therapist in the hope of a psychological 'pill' or treatment – all the power for the client's healing is vested in the therapist. Conversely, they may be suspicious of seeking professional help or sceptical about whether a therapist can help them, because the client's previous experience of the profession has not been positive. This problem is compounded if the client has been 'sent' to therapy by another professional, authority figure or significant person in their life. All this will create challenges about how to support the client to feel engaged in their own therapy because levels of trust and motivation are not high.

Obvious differences between client and therapist such as race, class, age and even style of dress may have an effect in the initial meeting between them, which could hinder the relationship. If the difference is experienced as something negative or if it triggers a response in the client, this will be an obstacle to building a working alliance. This has been described as 'the quality and strength of the collaborative relationship between client and therapist' (Horvath and Bedi 2002: 41, cited in Cooper 2008: 103). It's important that the therapist notices and considers any reactions on the part of the client that will need to be discussed with them.

A matrix of trust is at the heart of these dynamics, and if trust does not become a central feature in the therapeutic alliance very little psychological movement will take place. Clients come with varying degrees of trust and knowledge about the therapeutic experience. The quality of the therapist's respectful and engaged listening is a huge factor in creating safety and trust in the relationship. Training modalities may emphasize different kinds of interventions which build a trusting therapeutic relationship, but the attentive presence of the therapist and their ability to hear, stay with and acknowledge the client's emotional world with appropriate empathic responses is the foundation for this.

Contracting and motivation

Explicitly discussing with the client what they want from the sessions, and dispelling any misconceptions about what therapy does or does not offer, is essential. This discussion does not eliminate the inherent power dynamics within the relationship but it can make them more transparent and realistic. It also provides the opportunity for the client to be an active partner in the work rather than just a passive recipient.

All of the above points are linked with the motivation of the client to engage in the work, which is a key ingredient in successful therapy (Cooper 2008). Motivation means that the client has the desire to explore themselves and their inner world, which in turn provides the energy and openness needed to make this therapeutic journey in the presence of another.

If you are getting a sense whilst discussing the contract that the client is hesitant about being in therapy, it is useful to put this on the table for further exploration – for example, 'I'm aware it's your first time seeking therapy and I have a sense you have some concerns about it and maybe about being here with me.' If the client is able to acknowledge this it could afford a good opportunity to help them understand their underlying fears about talking to a stranger.

Self-reflection

This exercise is primarily intended to use for reflecting on a client's position but you could also use it to reflect on yourself in your own therapy.

Choose a client you are currently working with and consider the following statements:

- *They trust the therapeutic process.*
- *They trust you.*
- *They are motivated to engage in the work.*

Using a psychological 'barometer' which has 'readings' of: very strong, strong, middling, weak and ambivalent, consider which 'readings' best indicate the energy of your client in relation to the above statements. What is your learning from this?

All of the issues outlined above about trust, interpersonal dynamics and levels of motivated engagement are threads throughout the course of the therapy. They wax and wane through the therapeutic relationship and it is the therapist's responsibility to take notice of them and work with them when necessary. Sometimes the threads come visibly to the fore and need to be addressed directly. At other times they are beneath the surface of the relational dynamic but have implicit influences.

Challenging the client

In one sense, anything that happens in the therapy which sheds new light on the client, or stimulates and assists the client in reflecting further on themselves, can be regarded as a challenge (Culley 1991). The purpose of a challenge is to confront something, question something or query something that is habitual or buried within the client so that they can look again at themselves; even the simplest of reflections can do this. Nevertheless, there is a skill set which goes beyond reflective responses (Culley 1991) and provides a more specific and consciously challenging form of intervention. It means that the therapist's responses progress from merely staying with the client in the moment and tracking them, to inviting the client to explore new territory. Clients do also self-challenge as part of their journey and this is a sign of mature and responsible investment in their own growth.

When the challenge is actively led by the therapist it's important to bear in mind certain considerations. First, what is the therapist's motivation in challenging a client? Has the therapist a need to prove something about themselves and their competency? Making a challenge may also come from the therapist's need to wrest back control of the therapy if they are feeling out of their depth. Under these circumstances, challenging interventions are not in the best interests of the client.

Second, there is the ever-present issue of timing. Helping to determine what might be an appropriate time to make a challenge comes from having prior experience of your client. You will already have some knowledge of your client in terms of how reflective or not your client has been. In particular, you need to consider if the client is capable of thinking about and digesting something which is beyond their usual narrative or emotional presentation. In other words, how much does your client appreciate discovery about themselves or do they need to protect their self-image and current patterns of behaviour? Challenges can be disturbing, so is the client robust enough to be able to use an intervention which will make them question a view of themselves? If you are in any doubt about whether to challenge a client or not, it is better to wait, then take your ideas and questions to supervision for discussion.

All of these evaluations by the therapist sit alongside the question of whether the therapeutic alliance is strong enough at a particular point. If the alliance has a foundation of trust the client is more likely to experience a challenge from the therapist in a positive way, rather than as something which may be intrusive or hostile.

Having made a challenge, the therapist needs to notice its impact on the client. Sometimes the effect is immediate: they may ignore what you have said, make a distraction from the issue, or show a non-verbal body response – a facial expression or a body movement. If the intervention has been felt or perceived as some form of attack from the therapist, the client may not immediately show a response but it will still have an effect on the therapy and what is happening between you. A classic example is that the session seems OK on the surface but the client does not attend the next session. If this has occurred there has clearly been a rupture in the relationship, which the therapist will need to actively bring back to the room for discussion when the client reappears! For example, 'I wonder if you experienced me as too challenging in your last session and that left you with a lot of difficult feelings about yourself and about being in therapy?'

Examples

Here is a brief example from practice showing how the 'simplest' of reflections can have an important impact. A client I worked with came to a first session telling me all the things he believed he 'should' be – that word again! I responded by saying, 'You are very demanding of yourself.' Simple: not rocket science, not an interpretation of a deeper issue within himself, nor an interpretation about the origin of his inner self's demands, or how he might see me in the future or how he should be in the therapy. He had never considered himself as self-demanding. He thought he was rightly striving to do and be 'better'. My intervention confronted him because it offered a different view of himself and what he was doing to himself. It exposed a huge issue in his life that became woven into the fabric of the therapy in many ways. As we talked he revealed that he felt both seen and exposed by what I had said. For my part, I had not intended to deliberately challenge him as he had barely walked through the door of my room. I had hoped to be empathic towards some aspect of his inner torment, but the intervention had touched something deeper and more embedded in the fabric of his sense of self.

Another client I worked with was talking about her relationship with her partner and was describing him as clever, very successful in his professional life, and committed to his family. Whilst listening to her I did notice she didn't mention how he responded to her. If there had been a transcript of this part of the session, reading it would convey a sense that all was well in the relationship with her partner and in the home. However, as I was listening to her I wasn't convinced that this was the full picture. Her voice had no softness in it. It was as if she was reading a list of things that she was familiar with – like telling herself and me the same story. As she was a new client, I had to decide how much to challenge her. The ostensible reasons for seeking therapy had been because she was feeling lonely and had difficulty in making friends.

I had to weigh up: would it be better to wait and let the client come to realize that she had deeper feelings about her relationship or should I make a comment at this point? In the end I remarked on how she was presenting her story by saying 'I notice your voice seems flat as you are telling me about him.' She paused. I then got the sense of her thinking more deeply. She took some time before saying 'He can be a bit ... a bit, I don't know. A bit difficult sometimes.' This really was the start of allowing herself to think about and feel her deeper emotions towards her partner. She could have ignored or dismissed my observation. I think if I had said something more challenging such as 'It's difficult for you to tell me about how you and your partner relate to each other', it would have been too disturbing for her at that point and may have created a rupture in the therapeutic relationship. Also, if I had revealed my intuition that she was not happy about the quality of her relationship I think she would not have been ready to acknowledge this. I can't be certain of this, and no therapist can be 100 per cent sure about what the impact of what they say will be on a client. This is part of the unknown in the exploratory journey between the two therapeutic partners.

The skill of challenging a client is part of a continuum of how much to support them and how much to consciously stimulate them to think more deeply about themselves at any given time in the therapy. This always sits within the context of the therapeutic relationship itself – is the relationship strong enough at this point to allow for some disturbance, some uncertainty, and is the therapist robust and skilful enough to deal with any unforeseen response to their intervention? Be mindful that what you, the therapist, mean and intend when endeavouring to challenge is not always how the client experiences and perceives the intervention.

Self-reflection

Start by thinking about yourself:

- *Do you like to challenge others?*
- *Do you appreciate being challenged by another person?*
- *What is your natural inclination, to be more supportive or challenging?*

Think about when you have received:

- *a 'good' challenge from another person – what were the ingredients in it?*
- *a 'poor' challenge from another person – what made it unhelpful?*

When you have thought about the above, consider: what do you think you need as a new therapist, in order to develop this interpersonal skill?

The client's need for self-protection

Sooner or later as you work with your client, you will notice that the client has 'no-go' psychological areas or areas that are scantily explored. They may skip over some details that you think are relevant, shift their emotional state quickly when talking about an event or experience, talk about other people in the outside world but not about their own experience, regale you with humorous stories or recount dramatic events without emotion. There are also other mechanisms of psychological protection such as avoidance, denial, blaming others, using humour and making attacks on you, the therapist. There is also projection, which is seeing a trait or characteristic in another person that can't be admitted as belonging to yourself. Additionally, there is the defence of splitting, which in its blunt form is seeing people as either 'good' or 'bad'. It's an inability to hold complex views about people, to see that we are all a mixture of fluid and changing psychological energies and attributes.

A good indication that resistance is occurring is that you might find yourself responding in ways that are not characteristic of your working style: doing too much in the session, asking too many questions, feeling irritated, wanting to push, feeling disempowered, feeling sleepy or bored, and especially feeling shut out by the client. It is crucial that you acknowledge these reactions to yourself so that you can reflect further on them and that you take your experience of working with the client to supervision. It might feel as if you are a 'bad' therapist to admit in supervision that you felt bored or uninterested. Having the courage to do this, however, is likely to lead to a useful discussion about what might be happening.

Hycner (1993) emphasizes that resistance is a protective response on the part of the client to keep themselves safe. The question is, why does the client need to keep themselves safe whilst they are in the therapy room with you? Reasons for this may include:

- The client feels inherently unsafe with most people and in most places, and this is brought into the therapeutic relationship.
- The client feels unsafe because they are beginning to talk about difficult parts of their story with a concomitant reluctance and hesitancy to delve into their emotions.
- The client doesn't trust the therapist enough at this moment as there has been a rupture between you that has not been noticed or attended to; e.g. the therapist has made a 'mistake' but has not brought it to the table for discussion so the client is left feeling the need to protect their inner processes and experience.
- The client has experienced you as too intrusive or challenging in your responses.
- The therapy is going too fast.

Keep in mind that the client is anxious about something that they are experiencing within themselves, whether they know it or not. The therapist's task is to understand why the client might be holding back and to empathize with their fear about engaging at a deeper level. Being as empathic and as relational as you can be is the best way forward with a client in these situations.

For example, a client was telling me in a humorous manner about some of her dalliances with members of the glitterati. For a short time this blindsided me and thereby distracted me from focusing on what was of importance. Before she regaled me with these stories we had started to talk about very painful and disturbing experiences in her young life. It then dawned on me that we had shifted gear in the therapy and had stopped exploring her significant childhood experiences of witnessing traumatic domestic violence. When I realized what had happened over a couple of sessions (yes I had been pulled away – I admit it!) I said: 'We had been talking about your memories as a very young child and what you saw and heard in your family. I think it was becoming very frightening for you as you remembered your experiences and that made it very hard for you to keep on talking about it with me.' This helped the client to feel that I was trying to understand her need to protect herself from disturbing and painful memories, feeling and thoughts. In the therapy she showed courage and determination to continue to reflect on her own process, and our relationship was solid enough for us to be able to recommence the exploration and understanding of these events in her life. She was not primarily so much resistant as scared!

Trainee voice – how to work with a client's need to self-protect

'By the therapist "being present" they invite the client to take the space in any way they need to be.'

'Noticing, being aware, putting away the hypothesis (you hold) for another time.'

First time revelations

If a client tells you a part of their story which they have not told anyone else before, especially if the recounted experience describes a trauma, it is very significant for the client to do this, and for your relationship. Make a gentle enquiry about how the client feels now, 'post-disclosure', and if they have any regrets about disclosing it. For example, 'I'm really sensing that it took courage to share this painful experience with me. I wonder how you feel about doing that now?' or 'I wonder how you feel about my response to you as you told me this?' This might segue into a deeper exploration and dialogue about how the client experienced *you* as they revealed their story. If you did not make this enquiry about the revealed experience in the session you could bring it back in the following session, e.g. 'I'm aware in the last session you spoke about some very difficult and painful experiences; I wonder how you are feeling about being back in the room with me today?', and then wait for the client's response. Alternatively, you could wait and see if the client refers back to what happened in the previous session or how they felt afterwards.

Picking up a sense of an unspoken dynamic

If the counsellor has an intimation that something is going on in the relationship, a tentative enquiry such as 'I sense something is happening' or 'I wonder what's going on?' can work well at inviting the client to think about how they are in the therapeutic process in the moment. Reflective clients may go into deeper exploration after this prompt. A more direct and challenging intervention could be: 'I'm sensing a disconnection between us and I'm wondering if you are also experiencing this?' The client may deny this, but you have given a signal that they are in a therapeutic relationship in which you are open to talking about what may be going on between you.

Getting stuck/lack of contact

If you think the work is becoming stuck or your interventions are going nowhere, this is a sign of an unspoken communication between you. In the session you may have been trying hard to understand and make contact with a client, but to no avail. This is an indication that something is occurring within the client and between the two of you. For example, a therapist who is intending to convey empathy to a client who is crying in a session might say, 'I sense how sad you are right now.' If this intervention does not soothe the client or allow them to feel the therapist is with them, the therapist needs to take note of this response. If this is a repeated behavioural response by the client, the therapist needs to consider if and when to bring this to the client's attention.

One way to do this is to describe what you see: 'When I say that I notice your sadness you pick up the tissues and laugh at yourself in a dismissive way.' The therapist is indicating that they have seen the client attacking themselves. Depending on the client's response, the therapist could say 'and when your tears come, I have the sense that you don't want me to see them – it seems like you want to keep them private'. In making this comment, the therapist is inviting an exploration of why at that moment the client wants to keep the therapist at a distance. Timing is all, at this point. The critical consideration: is the client open and reflective enough and is there enough trust in the therapeutic relationship for the client to take the plunge and consider your comment? Sharing what you have seen may be sufficient for now.

Times of disruption

When there is a cancelled or non-attended session, either on the part of the therapist or the client, it is important to enquire about the client's experience of this. For example, 'I had to cancel at short notice last week. I wonder how you felt about me doing this?' Being over-apologetic rather than enquiring about the effect will block the client's experience and prevent what could be a useful exploration for the client.

Hints from the client

Clients frequently give hints about you and how the therapy is going. They do this in ways which are embedded and encoded in the narratives they bring. For example, a client I worked with frequently referred to a specific author she was reading who had written a self-help book. The client repeatedly commented that this author was marvellous and her book was so helpful. There were plenty of messages in that for me and about me which I had to talk to her about! Clients in recounting their dreams may have a figure in the dream who is an aspect of you or how they perceive an aspect of you. Listen in particular for fairy godmother/father figures or leaders and demons if you are aware that your client has issues about authority figures. The client may allude to you by speaking about other people in their narratives. Pay attention to stories where people: always let the client down, try to control the client, or are wonderful! All of these hints are possibly indicating how the client may already perceive you or how they unconsciously anticipate the way you might relate to them. Broad generalizations about the therapy and its effects are laden with implicit messages. For example, 'I didn't feel great after last week' might be a statement about how they actually felt if the session delved deep or was disturbing; however, it could also contain a message to you about how they are experiencing you, and the work you are doing together.

Trainee voice - from group discussion

Relational immediacy can be:

- *a very direct way to talk about the relationship and ask the client to enter into the relationship with us*
- *an invitation for the client to be unusually honest*
- *helpful in talking about 'us', which enables the client to see how they were in other relationships*
- *permission for the client to be angry in the knowledge that the counsellor will hold space for that and not dismiss it*
- *an opportunity to acknowledge errors and be reparative.*

The challenges include:

- *As therapists, needing to feel secure and congruent enough in the relationship to be able to use relational immediacy.*
- *Concern about containing what might come up for the client whilst remaining relational.*
- *Naming the fact that the feeling or what is going on in the relationship can feel scary.*

What helps the therapist to work in this way includes:

- *Being brave and taking small risks.*
- *Practising and feeling grounded in our work.*
- *Being aware of any countertransference coming up for us (see below).*
- *Using supervision/therapy.*
- *Trusting our feelings about the relationship and what is happening in it.*
- *Making sure we feel like there is a good enough 'working alliance' in the relationship.*

Using relational immediacy can be enough in itself to enhance understanding of the dynamic between the two therapeutic partners. It can also be a way of moving towards working more explicitly with transference dynamics if this is part of your working model.

Transference implications

A lot has been written about the unconscious process of transference since Freud's and Breuer's *Studies on Hysteria* was published in 1895. Some training programmes work explicitly with transference dynamics whereas others put less emphasis on working with them explicitly. Whatever the modality you are being trained in, it is worthwhile considering the question of who you might represent for the client at different points in the therapy. Jacobs (2003, available at: https://www.youtube.com/watch?v=LFlr0GmrGho) puts it well when he suggests that transference is not all-encompassing all the time. He recalls a client saying to him, 'There's a little bit of me that sees you as my father.' It was wonderful that the client was able to see how she was relating to him. He points out that the client was about the same age as himself and that this transference onto him was triggered by a forthcoming break in her therapy. The client had experienced breaks with her own father because he had been called up for duty in the Second World War, which was restimulating some anxiety in a part of her in the present. She was unconsciously transferring some buried feelings which she had felt about her father leaving into the present situation with her therapist. In these moments the client is not responding to who you are in the room, but is overlaying onto you an experience with a person from a different time and place – not necessarily the past. This causes confusion at best, or a potential rupture if these perceptions are not noticed and discussed. When working with a client it is useful to take the learning from Jacobs above and say 'a part of you sees me as ...'. This is far more accurate and less dogmatic.

What is regarded as a positive transference or overlay onto you may be initially helpful to the therapeutic process, for instance if, without being aware of it, the client experiences you like a favourite cousin. Conversely, if the client has had poor relationships with women, then working with a female therapist is likely to evoke unconscious feelings and thoughts about the therapist, which will filter through into the relationship. It is also possible that the same transference dynamics could occur with a male therapist. Transference is an unconscious process and the sex of the therapist is not as important as the hidden thoughts and feelings in the client that affect their perception of the therapist and which are being triggered in the room.

An example: a client who had been physically ill and was seeing a complementary practitioner at the same time as me, described the other practitioner as 'caring and supportive'. Until late into her long therapy with me, I had no sense that she experienced me as caring or supportive to her in any way. I was not troubled by this, but remained curious about how she might be perceiving me. It took a long time for her to let me in, to see that I was on her side too. By being able to stay with her negative feelings towards me, without trying to change them or reassure her that I was on her side, I enabled her to express her anger and disappointment with me. In her life she had felt very let down by her father and had ceased any contact with him for a long time. Her dead mother she remembered with sad fondness. She responded to the complementary therapist and myself by unconsciously perceiving something in each of us as being like an aspect of her parents. This particular relationship had the added element of what is known in psychoanalytic and psychodynamic terms as splitting (Howard 2010).

The dynamics did work through in the therapy. She had the courage and persistence to keep coming to see me, her 'not good enough' therapist, for about two years. Things began to change as she experienced that I did not tell her off, punish her or reject her for the feelings she expressed towards me. I could hear and allow her anger and disappointment towards me. More significantly, she began to experience that the world would not fall apart if she had angry feelings towards another person. This was a slow and evolving change in our interpersonal relationship over a long period of time. She remained working with her complementary therapist for most of the time she worked with me but the splitting also diminished, and I think she began to see and experience both of us in a more complex and realistic way.

Transference dynamics are everywhere in all relationships, but in therapy they do need to be noticed and thought about in the first place and addressed if they are creating a rupture or potential rupture in the therapeutic relationship. The degree of intensity in transference processes is complex. Sometimes a client's transference lens becomes quite rigid, e.g. you become 'completely wonderful' in the eyes of the client. This is an idealized transference. However, these unconscious dynamics can be immensely fluid and changing – a word, a look, an experience of you in the moment can change how the client perceives you or alter their assumptions about you in the room in that moment (Howard 2010).

Moving towards a transference interpretation

Interpreting transference dynamics needs to be done with care. If your training modality does not use transference interpretation, then it is not appropriate for you to try to use this skill. In addition, the relationship would also need a degree of solidity and for the client to have shown some capacity to reflect on themselves.

Using Jacobs' way of addressing a part of the client's self, you could make a tentative interpretation by saying 'I wonder if a part of you sees me as the teacher who always criticized your work?' or 'I wonder if a part of you sees something in me like your …?' or 'I wonder if something in me reminds you of …?' Using the phrase 'a part of' can feel less rigid than the more definite interpretation of 'I think you see me as your (mother) in this moment.'

If the client can contemplate this link between you and another, the discussion can proceed further to delve into the implications of these transference dynamics – who you have become for them and the implications of this overlay in the room. These discussions often reveal painful and difficult inner experiences of the client with others. Many transference feelings and thoughts towards the therapist come from the client's experience of people in authority and people who unconsciously arouse the client's unmet needs. Transference dynamics are also woven into experiences of idealization or denigration of the therapist, and how power, judgement and vulnerability are experienced in the relationship. Being able to hear that your client sees you partly as their withholding and judgemental mother without trying to deny this affords the opportunity for the client to bring this into the open. They can then bring their anger towards you, to be directly expressed. The therapist might think this is not a fair representation of themselves, but this is the client's view and their experience of being with you. It is invaluable for the client to be able to tell you this and for you to hear it without defending your position. Transference dynamics indicate deeper meanings about how the client is experiencing their relationship with you in that moment or at that time.

Through these dialogues which open up the transference you get a glimpse of the client's painful relational issues in their life. If the transference dynamic can soften and shift, it offers the chance that there might be a different outcome – i.e. that the client can express their experience of you without being mocked or punished, or having their experience denied. This new experience in the room may be transferred to the outside world so that the client begins to 'read' others' responses to them in a different way.

Countertransference dynamics – the ABD of it

As there are two people in the therapeutic relationship, it means that the therapist is also subject to feelings, thoughts and responses about their client and the work which is taking place. The therapist is not a robot, immune to the flux and flow of the relational dynamics between the two people. So learning to notice that you are experiencing a response to your client is the starting place for deeper examination of implicit dynamics both within yourself and in what is happening between the two of you. Some of this noticing will be within the therapy room. However, reflection after the session – while you write your process notes – and later in supervision may help to uncover more of the meaning of what you felt when you were in the room with your client.

A – Awareness

A good place to start is by developing your capacity to observe yourself during a session, taking note of what is happening in your body, noticing when you are sitting in a different posture, feeling a tension or pain in your body, when your breathing changes or a headache begins. All of these are part of a signalling or alert system suggesting that you are experiencing something that needs more scrutiny. Your body is trying to tell you about an inner emotional state that you are having in the room whilst working, but which you have not been aware of.

B – Begin to name the feelings and thoughts experienced

Recognize and allow yourself to identify what are you feeling in the room with the client, whether you think these feelings are justifiable or not. New trainees find it very difficult to acknowledge that they sometimes don't like an aspect of a client or find something about the client's behaviour or attitude difficult: for example, you might be feeling impatient with a client but find this hard to acknowledge. This kind of self-censorship means the therapist is missing an opportunity to learn more about themselves, and potentially about their client and what could be happening between the two of you.

Additionally, give attention to your thoughts: what are you thinking about? You might have an image, symbol, metaphor or story in your mind – fairy stories can be useful here. With one client I worked with, I kept on thinking about Cinderella. Such mental images could potentially be offering you an implicit sense of your client. What do you notice when the client has left – what still remains in you? It is very important to pay attention and to reflect on the possible meaning of your experiences and/or what they might suggest about the relationship.

Thus it is essential that you feel able to bring these new awarenesses to your supervision for further exploration. It is the case that good supervision may bring out awareness of how you feel and think about a client which had not occurred to you when working. This 'B' stage has both reflexive aspects in the therapy room and further reflective exploration in supervision.

D – Discern to whom it belongs

Having realized, for example, that you become irritated with a client when they say no-one gives them enough credit for what they do, you need to honestly assess, with the help of your supervisor and maybe your therapist, where your irritation originates. O'Brien and Houston (2000: 139) describe this as 'a continuum between mostly-about-me to mostly-about-the-other'. If it is the former it is likely that an experience of a person in your own life is unconsciously triggering this response in you towards the client. A possibility here is that you had a sibling who always wanted the limelight and praise in your family, which you disliked. This personal feeling, which you are not aware of, is causing you to hear resonances of your sibling in your client's story. In effect, your own personal material is being stimulated, creating feelings of irritation in you that are predominantly about you.

Casement (1985) made a major contribution to understanding how the client is trying to give the therapist information about how they feel through unconsciously impacting the therapist without actually explicitly telling them.

An example: a client I worked with who was going through many life changes – getting divorced, stepping away from a career because of illness and moving into a new area – came to a session in a buoyant mood. She was telling me about all the things on her list that she needed to do after she left the session. As I sat with her I became aware that I felt hugely sad. I quickly checked myself to see if I was conscious of any sadness in me before the session and also whether any of her story resonated with aspects of my life. I felt confident that the sadness I was experiencing was not my personal material. Consequently, I was able to empathically put back to her that, as I listened to her, there was a feeling of sadness as she was speaking to me. She was quite astounded when I said this and became silent; then her tears started to burst through her outward show of competent busyness. She was then able to take some ownership for the residual feelings of loss and sadness that she still had. The feeling of sadness was no longer in me. What happened between us is what is known as the unconscious mechanism of *projective identification*. Rowan and Jacobs (2002: 42) write: 'In projective identification, the therapist experiences feelings that are strange and alien and that do not appear to belong to the therapist. He or she is feeling something that the client is not prepared to feel and instead unconsciously projects into (not just onto) the therapist.' It means putting a feeling into the therapist because it is too painful to bear. The therapist's ability to discern and decipher how much of what they are feeling in the room comes from the client is a refined and valuable skill. It takes time to hone and demands much investment in the therapist's own personal journey.

Clients can also unconsciously induce in us ways of behaving towards them which can tell us about how they relate to others in the world and the response that others might make to them.

An example: a client tells you that virtually everything about their work situation – their colleagues and work system – is all wrong, and that they have good ideas about what would improve the situation but no-one is taking their views on board. As you sit and listen you become aware that you want to argue back and challenge them. Fortunately you realize that there are punitive and dismissive feelings emerging in you towards your client which you need to examine. Taking these strong responses to discuss with your supervisor helps you to understand that maybe this is a dynamic they evoke in people because of their own past experience. They were never heard or respected as a child and young person within their family environment, so they come to expect, consciously or not, that others will behave in a similar way towards them. This is the client's 'internal working model' (Bowlby 1969; Wallin 2007).

The client's unconscious expectation is then played out in the therapy setting. The therapist's impulse to challenge the client's ideas about the work situation has elements of a replay of the behaviours the client had experienced in their early family environment (Casement 1985). All of this was 'set up' by the client without awareness. Maroda (2010: 247) defines this enactment as 'repeating some scenario from the past within the therapy, without conscious knowledge or intent'. When the behavioural dynamic re-emerges in the therapy, if it can be noticed and its deeper meaning understood, there is the possibility of the cycle being broken. The therapist, having understood some of their unconscious part in the dynamic, could comment, 'There is something that makes me want to argue with you. It's like we are back in your family – no-one is listening – just fighting each other. Maybe you wanted to argue back but felt too frightened.' In doing this the therapist is understanding how an experience in the client's past is shaping the client's way of relating in the therapy room and the response they receive. If the therapist had not acknowledged and considered their own punitive response to the client, this dynamic would be played out again. Of course, the replay might occur in the therapy more than once. It can take many repeated unconscious throws of the dice in order for it to reconfigure in a beneficial way. However, when understood and worked through, these enactments can become aspects of growth for the client (Ginot 2007).

A caveat: it can be extremely rewarding to use the countertransference well for the good of the client's insight and growth. However, this needs care and skill developed over time with the aid of training and supervision. Howard (2010: 100) provides a salutary caution: 'Do not do anything while ever you feel a powerful urge to do so.' If you are in any doubt about what your response means for the client and your relationship, wait with them and reflect further rather than sharing your thoughts on the spot.

Working with difference

Looking out of my window, I notice the trees in the surrounding area. There is a variety of species in view. Even the trees from the same botanical species are different. I could just think in a general way that these trees need pruning. If I was a keen gardener and wanted to see the trees develop I would pay more attention to the environment where each tree grows, taking note of the quality of the soil, the distance from other trees, the surrounding land and if it was well kept, and the general environment and climate in the area. No tree is planted in exactly the same type of ground as its neighbour.

Examining our own bias

The starting place for working with difference and diversity is always the capacity to honestly examine oneself. Each person will have been imbued with the values of the family background and culture they came from. There may be elements of what we absorbed as a child which we might repudiate as an adult, but we need to be aware that they might still be unconsciously affecting us, at least in part. The work of psychologists Banaji and Greenwald (2013) identified the concept of hidden bias. In order to acknowledge and examine our own implicit bias there needs to be a willingness to be open about what might feel like uncomfortable aspects of ourselves. As with everything else we discover about ourselves that we don't like or sit comfortably with, we need to give time and reflection to understanding where and how this has developed and where it still exists in our relationships. When we begin examining our bias we are often looking at an old value system which is still impacting us. Acknowledging this is the first step to being able to self-challenge and to identify unconscious bias.

Self-reflection

Thinking about your own familial background, let yourself recall the values and beliefs that were strong in your background and culture. These beliefs may be explicit or not. (It doesn't mean that you agreed with them in the first place.) Make a list of these value systems. Try not to censor it.

Then, reflecting on your list, consider with curiosity:

- *What do I still believe in and give value to?*
- *What have I shed from the list and why have I done this?*

Looking at the list again – including the value systems you have 'shed' – ask yourself:

- *What do I still believe (or partly believe) that might be creating unconscious bias within me?*
- *How could I be more alert to elements of unconscious bias, assumptions or prejudice in myself?*

Example to consider

If you were brought up in a family with strong views about giving money and support to the less well off in society, and in your clinical placement – a cash-strapped charity – a client has revealed that they have a very good salary (and could afford to see a therapist in private practice), how might this knowledge of your client's financial position have an effect on you and how you relate to your client – even momentarily? What might go through your mind?

Understanding the client's perspective

From the 1990s the work of Professor Kimberllé Crenshaw, a lawyer, increased our awareness that experiences emanating from our social and cultural backgrounds impact upon our sense of identity and thereby our sense of well-being. These theories of intersectionality bring our attention to the impact of our backgrounds, particularly the fact 'that the major axes of social division in a given society at a given time, for example, race, class, gender, sexuality, dis/ability and age, operate not as discreet and mutually exclusive entities, but build on each other and work together'(Hill Collins and Bilge 2016: 4). These divisions enhance privilege for some but create hurt and pain for many other people. Turner (2021: 21) writes that 'What intersectionality allows us to do, therefore, is to bring to the surface, like a free diver, that which has increasingly been left in the depths of the unconscious, with multiple layers of difference being pulled to the surface and made visible for all to see.'

To date, the professions of counselling and psychotherapy are still predominantly white, middle class and female. Turner (2021) refers to how other authors – Dottolo and Kaschak (2016) and DiAngelo (2018) – explore privilege, whiteness, power, prejudice, racism and oppression in the therapy room. It is therefore important for the therapist to examine and acknowledge their own privilege or aspects of it. This is an important prerequisite to being able to pick up on and listen to the pain in clients who have experienced prejudice and bias. In addition, noticing when the client is self-attacking because of their own internalized bias is also something to be conscious of and to examine.

Self-reflection

In the spirit of exploration rather than self-judging, think about these questions:

- *In what ways are you privileged or have gained privilege?*
- *How could this privilege impede your capacity to be empathic with a client?*

Additionally, the theory of 'imposter phenomenon' (Clance and Imes 1978), which identified a person's experience in the workplace where they believed they did not have the intellectual ability to do the job, is now understood in a broader context – not just the working environment. I worked with a client who came from a 'humble' background and gained a place at a prestigious university to study medicine. Although this person was intellectually able, they always had a sense they did not deserve their professional success and felt they did not belong to the different socioeconomic group they had managed to enter by virtue of their education and current profession. In the therapy, the client struggled to find a sense of his own self-value. He was struggling with his own unconscious bias and unease concerning privilege, as well as experiencing some degree of 'imposter syndrome', both of these affecting his sense of self. Overtly he was a white professional male who had many privileges. His struggles in therapy were predominantly to find peace within himself.

Talking about differences: the 'obvious' and the 'not so obvious'

A possible place to start is at the first meeting, if there is an obvious difference between you. It is likely that at the clinical assessment at the agency, the client will have been invited to state whether they would like to work with a male, female or non-binary therapist. If the service has not been able to accommodate this request and if the therapist knows this preference has not been met, the onus is on the therapist to talk to the client about how they feel about being referred to you. This means gently enquiring whether the client has any reservations or fears about working with you, putting on the table the fact that the client's preference has not been accommodated by saying, 'You said you wanted to work with a male therapist but you have been allocated to me, a white woman, as your therapist. I wonder how you feel about this?' A client may be very anxious at the start of the work, especially if it is their first time seeking psychological help, and may minimize the difference or deny that it is bothering them. In the first instance, notice the client's response and stay alert to the possibility of these themes emerging later in the work, either explicitly or implicitly. You can also come back to them in the future for further dialogue.

Example: age difference

When I first started work in private practice I found myself to be younger than many of my clients. With some the age gap was not very wide, but one client was an older woman with a daughter of a similar age to me, so there was an age gap of a generation. One of her reasons for coming to therapy was because of her difficult relationship with the daughter, which was causing her distress. Herein lay ripe material for both transference and countertransference dynamics which could impede the therapy. I was concerned that she would not trust me enough to reveal what she needed to talk about, as perhaps she didn't think I had enough experience to work with her. This was my anxiety about working with her given that I was a young and newly qualified therapist. I also wondered if she would unconsciously relate to me as if I was like her daughter, which could inhibit the work. Admitting my own feelings and pondering the impact of the age difference between us gave me the confidence to reaffirm that I was after all qualified and had the clinical experience to work with her. Having gone through this process within myself, I decided that it was important to discuss the very obvious age difference between us when it was alluded to or came up in the therapy. A few sessions later the client arrived distressed as a result of a conversation she had had with her daughter. Whilst telling me about this she made a very swift passing comment about young people not understanding what she had done for them (she was probably alluding to her other children as well). Here was the material right in the room. It was important for me to talk to her about it. I enquired about how she felt working with a younger therapist, which gave rise to a fruitful conversation between us. She was initially very reluctant to say that she thought I could not handle the material, especially about how she felt about her daughter – all of this accompanied by comments that 'policemen look younger all the time'. With encouragement and further exploration she was able to admit her reservations about me because of my age: would I understand how she felt? Maybe I thought her daughter was right. Through this dialogue between us the 'elephant in the room' was no longer hidden. I feel fairly certain that if we had not spoken about this difference the therapy would have been less effective and maybe would have ended, as she would not have felt free to openly say how she felt about her daughter and their relationship in my presence.

In the above examples the differences between client and therapist are obvious, but this is not always the case. In listening to your clients' stories you, the therapist, may become aware of a 'hidden' difference between you – class, sexual orientation or religious beliefs, to name but a few. A key consideration is: should a hidden difference that the therapist has seen be introduced into the therapy if the client has made no reference to the issue? This would be a direct intervention on the part of the therapist.

Being able to talk about difference between you and your client is another key developmental step for the new trainee.

Trainee voice – the challenges of working with difference

The following issues were identified and discussed in the training group. This is what was recorded after discussion:

1 *Our countertransference/internal reaction towards the specific diversity issue – getting in the way, especially guilt from our own background (privilege).*
2 *The therapist's fear of doing things badly/clumsily which then might lead to a rupture.*
3 *The client's feelings (a sense of shame) because of difference, creating difficulty in talking about the issue (which can be a transference reaction).*
4 *The challenge of timing – particularly with invisible differences. So, naming obvious difference early, gently and tentatively, and invisible difference and diversity when it comes up in the client's agenda. Not forcing the client to explore. Inviting the client to be curious when the client alludes to something about it.*
5 *The client may not be ready to talk about the issue of diversity (the therapist could acknowledge the client's difficulty and relationally explore it).*
6 *Being aware of a difference in power between client and counsellor – the client may reveal everything and the therapist nothing about themselves.*
7 *Does the therapist disclose that they share an invisible difference with the client? The emphasis is on the safety of the client and their therapeutic process, not about the therapist.*
8 *If the client asks a direct question relating to a difference between you, the therapist could enquire, 'What does it mean for you to know this about me?'*

Trainee suggestions for ways to overcome the challenges in working with difference:

- *Recognizing our assumptions and negative feelings and where they are coming from – self-development (doing work on ourselves).*
- *Using relational skills tentatively, being very gentle and attuned to the client.*
- *There is always difference – we just don't always know what the difference is and how it is impacting on the client. We have to find a way as therapists to open the door for them to discuss the difference if there is one that matters to them.*

One of the concluding remarks from the group discussion is: if we bring difference to the conversation we show we are not afraid of discussing it.

Rupture and repair

Ruptures happen. Most micro-ruptures happen when we misunderstand the client. Despite this clients generally give us another chance to 'get them'. However, sometimes more serious ruptures may emerge. These may develop if we have seriously misunderstood what the client is trying to tell us, which is then compounded by the fact that we haven't picked up on the signs that something has happened between us. If this is the case, the client is left with difficult feelings which may trigger a resistance on their part to the therapy at this point, or a shutting down during the session. These are the client's protective reactions to what they are experiencing as a failure in the relationship with you.

At other times, the client may hear something in our tone of voice that sounds like a judgement or a telling off. If this has any resonances to their past they will be very sensitive and reactive to these tones. It may be their own perception of us rather than something we were actually trying to convey. This is always difficult to determine because the therapist also has an unconscious process and relates to their client in ways they are not always aware of. What the therapist needs is the alertness to sense that there has been a change in the relationship, and to consider where this might come from or what has contributed to it.

The therapist may make overt mistakes, such as forgetting a client's appointment, being late for the session or calling the client by the wrong name. Less obvious mistakes may include the therapist inappropriately disclosing something of their own history which takes away from or diminishes the client's story in the room, or distracting the client because the subject matter is uncomfortable for the therapist, or acting out their own unconscious processes which may or may not have been stimulated by the client's material. Karpman (1968) suggests that we can switch between different roles in a relationship: namely, the rescuer, victim and persecutor. Adopting any of these roles when working with a client, especially the persecutor role, may put the therapy in jeopardy.

No-shows during a course of therapy are significant. If a client has attended regularly and punctually and then cancels (especially at short notice) or comes late to the session, this is likely to reflect some ongoing process. Maybe the psychological work is going too fast for the client, so that they are feeling exposed both to themselves and to you, or they are feeling too disturbed by the psychological material that is emerging, or they have hit a wall and don't want to explore the wall or beyond it. This needs to be addressed as soon as the therapist notices this change. Going too quickly or exploring too deeply with a client are basically failures to judge the readiness of a client to work at a deeper level, or the robustness of the therapeutic relationship in holding them in this process of exploration. Consequently, poor timing of interventions can cause the client to batten down the hatches or take flight from the therapy.

Self-reflection

- How easy is it for you to acknowledge that you may have contributed to a rupture in the therapy?
- How easy is it for you to reflect on a therapeutic 'mistake' with curiosity and a mind open to learning without losing faith in yourself?

Ruptures can be repaired, but in order for this to happen they first need to be addressed (Safran et al. 1990: 159, cited in Cooper 2008: 121). This requires the therapist to recognize in the first place that the client is presenting in a different way or that a connection has been lost or changed in the relationship. Noticing this is a crucial step to finding a way to repair the relationship. It might be that only after presenting the client in supervision do you realize that a rupture has happened. But having gained this realization it's not too late for you to attempt to repair the relationship, when you meet the client again.

A good place to start is to share your sense of the relationship and invite your client to think as well. For example, the therapist may say, 'It seems that something has changed between us in the last few minutes' or 'I sense our connection is different today.' The therapist is signalling that, from their viewpoint, there has been a change in the psychological temperature in the room and is inviting the client to give some attention to this fact and to comment on it. Clients can respond to this by denying any change, or they can begin to ponder that there is a difference although they may not be able to articulate what it is. For a reflective client who feels secure with you, it provides an opportunity to speak out to you about their current experience of being with you. For some clients this is immensely important and their first such opportunity.

Having made the invitation to reflect on and discuss the changed dynamic between you, if the client is struggling to articulate what is going on, the therapist could offer an empathic suggestion about the cause of the change by saying, for example, 'I wonder if it's because I didn't really understand what you were saying about your father?' This gives the client some time to ask themselves if they recognize that your intervention did not sit right with them. The client may not actually have been aware that they were reacting to your intervention. If the client can acknowledge that they did not like your intervention, then there is the possibility of a repair of the relationship and even a deeper exploration.

For example:

Client: Yes. It did feel a bit ... not OK. I'm not sure ... But you said you thought I resented my Dad. I don't. I feel hurt by him.
Therapist: I really didn't understand you. I wonder how you feel about this?

The therapist has taken responsibility in the above exchange for their part and offers this up for discussion. The client could become scared at this point and go into a compliant or placatory mode with the therapist if this is their habitual response to authority when they feel hurt. The therapist needs to reflect this back to the client. 'Perhaps you feel you can't tell me that I got it wrong for you too?' This invites the client to reflect again on how they feel, which may uncover patterns of relating that are habitual and familiar to the client, which are now being replayed in the therapy room. This time, the therapist's interested enquiry can give the client the chance to break a pattern because the client is encouraged to express their experience directly with the person they feel misunderstood them. Persisting with this relational enquiry could lead to a breakthrough into an honest expression of how they feel about you – for example:

Client:	You didn't get how hurt I feel about being let down by him. I have hidden it for most of my life and tried to put it away but I was trying to let myself speak about it. I've been angry about him most of my life but it's kept my hurt away. You kept talking about my anger. It's my hurt that matters most now.
Therapist:	So maybe you are angry with me because I didn't understand you.
Client:	Um, a bit. I thought you would understand.
Therapist:	It's really important that you can say that to me.
Client:	Yes. I am angry that you didn't see my pain. That's what has happened all my life. I expected a therapist to see that.
Therapist:	I can really hear you feel I let you down and I can hear your anger towards me about this.

The client made a highly significant step in conveying how they are feeling directly to their therapist. The therapist, by acknowledging their 'mistake' and encouraging the client to directly express what they felt, has gone a long way towards restoring trust in the therapeutic partnership and process. That might be enough in itself for the client at this point, or it could lead to exploration of the client's patterns of relating, including possible transference dynamics in the client's life.

Failure to repair a rupture may come from the therapist not recognizing that a rupture has happened, but blindly trying to plough on. A result of this could be that the client doesn't show up for a session or they leave the therapy. The therapist, especially if they are a new trainee, might be too anxious to admit in supervision that they did something to create a rupture in the relationship.

Avoiding talking about a rupture puts the therapeutic alliance in peril. It takes courage and confidence to work directly with this situation because you are working with the dynamic between the two of you. With new trainees there may be a tendency to try to repair the relationship by apologizing too readily for the mistake they made, instead of allowing the client to express how they feel and think about what you did. A rupture could be a way of illuminating an issue in the client's life that needs attention and which may have remained hidden if the rupture had not been explored. So take heart and look at the issue honestly, with the support of your supervisor.

Whether you make its dynamics explicit or not, a good therapeutic relationship can be a significant force for healing in a client's life. Most hurt we suffer comes out of experiences in dysfunctional or abusive relationships. The therapeutic relationship at its best can help restore confidence in relationships between people, as the client has had a very different experience with you. It provides a space for a client to experiment with telling their truth to another person in a non-judgemental environment. In addition, being able to engage in 'you-and-I' talk can provide a new model for the client of how to communicate and have dialogue with others outside the therapy room. For some clients, the main reparative element of the therapy is the experience of being in a respectful and empathic relationship, which restores something inside the client's own self and helps to rebuild their sense of self-worth.

11 Endings in therapy

Ending a session

For a new trainee it can feel challenging to bring an end to a therapy session. Trainers and supervisors will have given guidance about this and there will have been experience in personal therapy and personal development groups in training. However, actually making an ending with the first client(s) is daunting. There are practical and psychological aspects of making a clear and safe ending with a client.

The therapist needs to have an awareness of time. Be clear about when the session started and the time the session is due to end – i.e. after 50 minutes. If it's possible to start on the hour that will help keep time accurately. Having a time device, e.g. a clock which is visible to the therapist, is useful. The therapist will learn the art of being able to discreetly check the time with a slight movement of the head or eyes. Some therapists have a clock which is visible to both parties. If this is the case the responsibility for keeping time still rests with the therapist. In a placement trainees often work within one-hour time slots, so if they do not finish on time and vacate the room they are causing an inconvenience and difficulty for the therapist (and their client) who will be using the room afterwards.

Keeping time is also a safety feature for a client. They will know how long they have got. Their psyche will start getting a sense of how much time they have in the session and how far they can travel into their process. If there is a varied and unpredictable time length to the session this will create anxiety. Timekeeping is an essential boundary for the work and a part of the therapeutic contract with the client. It needs to be respected.

The psychological challenges for the new trainee centre around issues of trust and authority. There can be strong responses around ending a session if a client is distressed. The therapist needs to trust that this may be part of the client's journey and that all stops on the journey (like at the end of a session) are not always easy, but that does not mean that the journey can't continue after a break between sessions. Unless the client is describing suicidal ideation and/or intent the therapist needs to trust the capacity of the client to take care of themselves well enough after a session and to trust the therapeutic process.

Consequently, the therapist's attitude to holding their authority in order to make and keep the time boundary touches their personal processes. If they are uneasy about asserting boundaries there will be a conflict between what the therapist needs to do, i.e. end the session, and a fear or inability to do it. As well as talking about this difficulty in clinical supervision, the deeper elements of their process are best reflected upon in their own therapy. The therapist needs to believe in the rightness of making an ending on time and know how to use their voice purposefully to do this – i.e. strengthening the sound and quality of the voice and being clear in the wording used to end the session. Clients need an unambiguous message and an unapologetic one.

One of the main 'mistakes' new therapists make with ending a session is doing an overall summary of the session which is too general (and usually too long). It is more appropriate to let your client know that you understand where they have arrived at the end of the session by making an empathic acknowledgement of what the client is feeling or still thinking about. For example, working with a client who has split with a partner and is still very emotional at the end of the session, the therapist could acknowledge this by saying, 'We need to end, although I can see that you still have a lot of strong and confused feelings about your ex-partner.' You are demonstrating that you see the client's reality and are empathically reflecting their experience, but reaffirming that the session will end.

Another 'mistake' is to try and make things better for the client in some way – going for the positive or putting what I call a 'pink bow' on the client's situation. Doing this can diminish the client's experience and could make them feel that they have to look on the bright side. If there is a serious mismatch between what the client is feeling and what the therapist has said they will leave feeling misunderstood.

Conversely, being so concerned about a client who is distressed or disturbed at the end of the session that there is an apology for closing the session implies that the therapist believes the client does not have enough resources to survive the ending of the session and the forthcoming week.

Lastly, opening up a new area to explore in the last minutes of the session is not helpful and can leave the client feeling unsatisfied. Even if the client has hinted at a new area for exploration in the closing minutes of the session, this needs to be noted by the therapist rather than acted upon. Bear in mind what the client has said, then wait and see if they bring it back to the work next week.

Ending a session online poses the question of who actually presses the button first and if it actually matters. Overall it's best to replicate as much as possible of 'in the room' practice in the online context, so the therapist closing the online room is akin to the closing of the door by the therapist.

Planned breaks as an ending for now

For some clients a long-planned break by the therapist can feel like the ending of the course of therapy. Defining what a long therapeutic break is can be difficult, but as a rule of thumb I would say that more than two or three weeks without therapy is a long break. Clients with issues concerning abandonment and loss may keenly feel the absence of their sessions, and this interval may seem endless. They can become very angry or distraught about the break. Even if the therapist rightly enquires about the client's feelings about their break the client might deny its importance. Therapists need to have breaks but need to be able to bear any resulting anger, disappointment or resentment from their clients. What the therapist does is to take a break and come back to their clients. Clients should be reminded that a break is not an end but a temporary suspension of contact that will be restored.

Referrals as an ending

It is likely that at some point during your placement there will be a discussion in supervision about whether to refer a client on to another therapeutic or support service. There are several reasons why a client might need to seek help outside the agency and/or need a referral:

1 Longer therapeutic input. If the placement offers short-term work (up to 12 sessions) it could become apparent that either the client has not worked through the original issue which brought them to therapy or the work has revealed another psychological area for examination that has become difficult or painful for the client. Some placements have a list of other agencies or services that can be given to a client who wants to continue in therapy. In these circumstances the placement may leave it up to the client to pursue these other services rather than making a referral on the client's behalf. This is usually discussed with the client towards the end of their therapy.

2 Specialist input. Most placements offer generic counselling for adults. Clients who experience specific difficulties such as eating disorders, addiction or severe trauma may need specialist therapeutic input. This information is not always known or disclosed at the assessment or start of the work.

3 The need for GP involvement or a psychiatric assessment. If the client's mental health deteriorates and they need care through the statutory services, making contact with their GP is the gateway to obtaining further provision for the client. If the client needs to be seen by a psychiatrist this needs to be actioned by their GP.

4 The availability of other support, e.g. special interest groups or facilities such as occupational health services or social support services.

5 On very rare occasions it may emerge that the original therapist may not be the most appropriate for the client to work with – usually because there is a special issue which is outside the scope of the therapist's knowledge and competency or because there may be a therapist who speaks the language of the client who could offer this expertise. Also, a therapist may go off sick or suddenly leave the agency.

In all of the above situations, discuss any concerns in supervision. Then the therapist needs to talk with their client about the next step for getting external mental health or support and services. Sometimes the client has enough confidence to seek these additional services for themselves. In other cases it feels supportive to have the involvement of the placement in making the referral on their behalf.

If the placement is making the referral, discuss with the client:

- what has been proposed as a way forward
- whether they give consent for the referral to be made
- whether they know the procedure for how the referral will be made and who will be involved in it, e.g. the agency manager
- the referral letter which will be or has been written on their behalf – check that the client has seen a copy of this letter and agrees to it.

If the client becomes concerned or changes their mind about being referred this necessitates further discussion. Transparency is crucial, otherwise trust will be broken.

Unfinished and messy endings

Sometimes a client disappears from the therapy without trace. This is challenging and can be worrying for the therapist, especially if the client had been vulnerable or very troubled in the previous session. It leads to a lot of speculation about what has happened to the client. A new therapist can become caught in their own self-recrimination about not doing good work with their client. However, there will be some clients who leave for no apparent reason. Discussing in supervision what may have been happening in the work and in the client's life may help the therapist to consider the possible meaning of the client's action. These unexpected disappearances can be professionally and emotionally difficult to deal with.

Occasionally, a therapist may also disappear without a trace. A colleague recounts that a client of hers had a previous therapist who suddenly vanished. The client had turned up to the former therapist's house and had no response to ringing the doorbell. What was worse was that the client never heard from the therapist again or anyone connected with them. This was extremely disturbing for the client and made her next therapy sessions (she had the courage to continue) very insecure for a long time. Professional organizations are now requiring that their members make a professional will, i.e. an agreement with a professional colleague or a solicitor to ensure that clients are notified if they become seriously unwell or die, and that clinical notes are taken care of.

With a messy ending there is a lot of to-ing and fro-ing, with the client forgetting a session or trying to move the ending date, or having a break before the ending as a mini practice of being without the therapist. A client may even have a crisis in their life before the planned ending of the therapy. The therapist should take note of these actions and discuss their possible meaning with the client, and keep to the schedule of the therapy and its ending date.

Making an ending with your client

The first time a therapist makes an ending with a client (maybe this is also with their first client) there can be feelings of anxiety about doing this. The therapist needs to allow some time to contemplate the meaning of this ending and how to do it well – it is another milestone – rather than letting it creep up with no time to think about what it might mean to both therapeutic partners. It is significant, particularly if a bond was made between therapist and client and the client really engaged in the work. It is likely that the therapist will remember this client for a long time in their career.

Endings are imbued with layers of meaning. They are part of the continuing cycle of birth, change and death. How the therapist feels about endings will impact their attitude to making endings with a client or specific clients.

Self-reflection

To be useful, this exercise takes time – maybe 30 minutes – so allow yourself the space to do it. You need a large piece of paper, and pens or coloured pencils are also useful.

Start by drawing a line on the paper – straight or curving. This will represent your timeline. Put some age markers on the line: 10, 20, 30, etc. from your birth up to the present. Then ask yourself, 'What have been the significant changes for me in my life?' Mark on the timeline at the appropriate age marker all the significant endings in your life – changes of homes, schools, friends, jobs, career, other significant events in your life and losses of people or pet companions. Then look at what you have drawn and go back and remember as best you can all the emotions and thoughts evoked by the particular endings on your life journey. Jot down some words underneath each experience.

Look again at what you have drawn. Which events or experiences on the timeline seem most significant and why? Consider if these endings share something in common. Are there common psychological themes or emotions associated with these experiences? Take some time to notice how you are feeling now. Maybe jot down some thoughts or remarks that may need further consideration.

When you have taken some space from this personal exploration, consider what you need to be aware of when working with your clients. Make a note of anything that may be significant to working with clients in the present or future.

Dynamics in endings

When working in a placement, it is unlikely that there will be much room for negotiation about the ending of the therapy in a service that offers short-term therapeutic contracts. Even in placements that offer medium-length contracts of six months to a year there is still a therapeutic finishing line that will be approaching. Whilst the client may be able to review at different times whether they want to continue or not, they do not have the overall power to determine how long the work will last. In this way the client can feel powerless over what is happening to them as they approach the looming end date, especially if they want to continue with the work.

On the other side, it can be difficult for a new trainee to 'let go' of their client if they consider that the client is not ready to go – that there is more work to be done or if the client is still in a difficult position. This may pull at the heartstrings of the new trainee who has compassion for another's suffering in life. There may also be a sense of guilt or failure in the therapist. This comes from an inner part of the therapist's self which holds (usually unconsciously) a sense of themselves as the saviour/rescuer/healer that has not helped the client enough.

It can also be difficult to let a client go if a good attachment has been made with them. There is a sense of loss for the therapist as well. I think this has very little to do with whether the work was short term or long term, although long-term work may intensify the feelings about the ending. Clients impact thera-pists as well. They share parts of themselves and the therapist travels with them on their journey. Creating such a bond means at some point the loss of the attachment will be felt.

On the other hand, there may be a difficult ending if the client has expressed overtly or implicitly negative or aggressive responses to the therapist. This can leave a bad taste or mixed emotions in the therapist.

Endings as a replay of relational patterns

The ending of the therapy can also illuminate an element of the client's rela-tional patterns. If endings are a major theme in the client's emotional life and they have had a number of difficult and painful endings, the prospect of the forthcoming ending with their therapist will be highly charged. How the client will leave the therapeutic relationship is likely to replicate earlier endings they have been involved in. Some clients can only leave a relationship by having a fight. If this plays out unconsciously in the work, it could cause something to happen which leads to a rupture between therapist and client in the closing sessions. The client has got the fight they need in order to leave the therapist, and this is the only way they know how to leave a relationship. In other cases they may leave before the therapist formally ends the work with them. These forms of endings can be painful on both sides. If they can be anticipated and spoken about there may be a chance for making a different ending.

Avoiding the ending

Clients with a history of avoiding or escaping endings are likely to make the ending as unimportant as they can. It's a 'ciao' ending, not one involving thought and emotional processing. It is the therapist's job to invite them to recognize that an ending will take place and that somewhere inside the client's self there is a deeper emotional and cognitive response to it. Invite the client to face the ending in their therapy, i.e. to allow time for the idea of the ending to sink in, to allow space for their feelings and thoughts about it and to allow themselves to consider if it is or will become a repeat of their usual relational patterns. Within training programmes much of the thought about endings is left to supervision when the issue crops up.

Trainees can also avoid or minimize the reality and the therapeutic importance of making an ending with a client. They might do this by ignoring or giving scant attention to the fact that the contract is coming to a close. This is typically done by forgetting that the work is ending the following week, neglecting to bear in mind the number of sessions left in the agreed contract and not alerting the client to this reality. This means therapist and client have little time to discuss the ending and what it means for the client. It is essentially minimizing the importance of the relationship.

Forgetting means there is little opportunity to take time to invite the client to take stock of what has been important to them in the work, what remains unfinished and if the client needs information or support to seek further therapy. Inherent in this 'forgetting' is that there is no time for evaluative feedback about where the therapeutic relationship has reached, including what helped the client and what was not so helpful. On a practical level, with a placement contract there will be little or no time to complete any paperwork, e.g. for filling in feedback forms or outcome measures, or to discuss referral procedures inside or outside of the placement and to collect final fees or donations which were agreed at the time of the client's assessment. Above all there is no space for the client to bring their feelings and thoughts about the end of the work and the relationship to the room and have them heard.

In the worst scenario the therapist has not made explicit at the start of the last contracted session that the work will end when the session is over. This leaves the client open to being surprised at best and shocked at worst, if they too have edited out the fact that the contract is over at the end of the session. The therapist's unprocessed relational history of endings can also silently impact the work. Avoidance, denial and omission are unspoken elements in either or both parties.

Self-reflection

Select a client that you have some unease about ending with. Think about:

- why you find it difficult to end with this particular client
- why the client might be finding the ending of therapy difficult.

On reflection, what seems most significant in the above? How could you use the understanding to facilitate a better ending experience for the client?

Things to do to facilitate an ending of the therapeutic work

1 Dates. Be clear in your mind when the contract will end. Have a countdown in your head to keep the number of remaining sessions in mind. Share the countdown of at least the last three sessions with your client.

2 Prepare. Remind your client, in the penultimate session, that the next session will be the final one.

3 Signal plan. Confirm that you will have time in the last session to think about the work you have done together and where the client is at, and to complete any research forms (if the placement uses them).

4 Advance discussion. Near the end of the work, especially if the work has been long term, discuss with your client the meaning of this ending with you.

Self-reflection

Internally you can:

- *Write an inventory of what strengths or insights you think the client has, that can help them carry on their journey after the end of the therapy.*
- *Write an inventory of what you have learned as you worked with this client. Acknowledge any growing edges that have come out of this particular piece of work.*
- *Consider with hindsight what you might have done differently, and bring these reflections for discussion in supervision.*
- *Consider your feelings about closing the work with this client. Allow yourself to feel what you might consider unacceptable qualities, such as relief.*

Things to do in the ending session

Start the session by reiterating that the work is at an end. Then invite the client to tell you how they are and help them to evaluate the meaning of the work for themselves. If you feel comfortable with it, acknowledge any strength or attribute that you have seen in the client. This can be expressed in words or through an image or a metaphor. I said to one client, 'I can see how your warrior spirit has given you energy to fight through the hardships and struggles of your life.' These statements have to be delivered with complete sincerity and integrity, and not as a means of softening the blow of the ending. If the ending is very challenging and the client aggressive, it may be best not to offer any 'positive' comments as they are unlikely to be received well and could be construed as patronizing or false.

For the closing of the session consider what gesture, if any, is appropriate to offer the client, e.g. a handshake, taking them to the front door to say goodbye, if this is not the usual practice. Above all be definite about the end of the session time and the end of the work. Loopholes or ambiguity do not help the reality of the situation. Both of you need to acknowledge the 'good bye' and be able to bear the loss.

Endings in general

The unknown. The therapist does not know what state the client will be in after the work has ended. If the client has completed the contract but is still in a vulnerable state the therapist has to live with this uncertainty about this person. This can feel very difficult. The therapist may feel out of control with endings which have been imposed in some way, e.g. through time limitations or contractual elements. Unexpected or abrupt endings where the client doesn't show up and there is no information or message from the client can feel like a rupture and leave the therapist with a sense of being left hanging. The therapist may experience this disappearance as an attack on themselves and the work. Feelings of being out of control and/or being incompetent can emerge.

Resonant endings. The therapist will have their own experience of endings in their life. Many of these may come from endings which are part of the common transitions of life. What the therapist feels about endings in their own life will have an impact – consciously or unconsciously – on how they see, welcome, avoid or are ambivalent about endings in therapy. If there is a strong identification with the client's history of endings this can impact upon how the therapist feels about work with a particular client coming to an end. It's important that the therapist is aware of their own responses.

Existential meanings. In an ending something is let go of. This process can feel like a death – big or small. At times this is welcomed or experienced as an alleviation of a burden or demand. At other times this is an enormously painful loss.

Ending with some clients can feel like a relief if the work has been very difficult or the therapeutic relationship challenging. It is important to acknowledge this as a normal response rather than seeing it as a failure. All therapists at times in their careers can experience this. Talking about and sharing the experience in supervision may offer other viewpoints about the meaning of the ending with the client which supports the therapist in doing this necessary part of the therapeutic work.

The ending of your own training

As the formal training draws to a close it is important for the therapist, individually and as a member of a training group, to acknowledge, think about and discuss what the ending means personally and collectively. There are often pressures of completing assignments and portfolios in the last term that can cloud the fact that the training will stop. However, making an ending with the training group is a crucial event to acknowledge. The training group will have shared and witnessed the milestones of personal and professional development with you. Consequently, there can be intense feelings of loss connected with the ending of the course. The training programme and the organization will have provided structure and focus in the therapist's life and there may be fear of a looming gap. There is the actual and symbolic leaving of the training organization or 'family' – for all its advantages and challenges. Owning the thoughts and feelings about this ending and saying goodbye is a mark of respect for the journey that has been travelled together through rough and smooth.

A big question when finishing training is: should personal therapy end? The obligatory therapy hours required by the training organization have been completed so it might feel like a natural break to complete with the training therapist at the same time. This is now a very personal decision to make. It's important to consider and anticipate the balance of support and pressure after the training finishes. This is best discussed whilst still in therapy so that there is time to think about it, especially if important psychological processes are alive in the work.

Whatever you decide is best for you, keep in mind that our psyches and our personal processes do not always work on the same timescale as training time. If you have a break at this point it is likely that at a later time in your career you may go back into therapy – this time of your own volition! We always have elements in ourselves that get triggered by the work, not to mention the journeys of our own lives; so seeing therapy not only as a training obligation may lead us to take up the therapeutic journey again at a later stage. Some therapists do their most important personal work after training has ended because they are doing it for themselves, not because they have to do it.

The ending is also a time of celebration. There has not been a trainee I have known who has not been delighted to be done with all the work of the assignments, assessments and exams which have been part of their training programme. Even those who like study are glad to be released from the scrutiny of these elements and to be able to read books and develop themselves in their own time and at their own pace. Time is one of the gifts that can be reclaimed once the therapist has qualified. Additionally, the therapist is now released from the costs of the training course and all its additional financial demands. The third component hopefully regained is the increase in energy for everyday living and revitalization. It is right to celebrate the return of these aspects of life as it acknowledges the investment that has been made over the years of training.

Certification, accreditation and registration

On successful completion of training, the training organization will make a request for the formal certification of the qualification on the therapist's behalf. The qualification will be awarded by an examination board – the examination board of the training programme or from the awarding university for the course. These certificates or degrees are the proof of the therapist's competency to practise as either a counsellor or psychotherapist.

As counsellor training is shorter, the counsellor will continue to accrue clinical hours after the end of training in order to be eligible to apply for individual BACP accreditation when they have gained 450 clinical hours under supervision. This usually takes at least a year and a half or two years after training. The counsellor will make this application for accreditation; it does not go through the training organization.

For psychotherapy training programmes, at the point of completion the training organization will put the therapist forward for both the qualification (e.g. diploma/advanced diploma or degree) and for registration as a full member (rather than trainee member) of the professional organization (e.g. The UK Council for Psychotherapy (UKCP)). The psychotherapist will join one of the colleges of the UKCP depending on the membership of their training organization. For example, I am a member of the UKCP's HIPC (Humanistic and Integrative College).

These final acts of closure of the training and acquiring the status of a professional counsellor or psychotherapist are deeply symbolic as well as practical. They give great delight to the therapist. Trainers are also very pleased to see the success of their trainees.

12 The post-qualifying year

Newly qualified

Upon qualifying the therapist is confirmed as competent and safe to practise in private practice (should they wish) under supervision. I remember a tutor saying to my training group when we were in the final stages of training that it takes about five years post-qualifying to really learn and embed the skills and ability to work therapeutically. I think there is a lot of wisdom in this. Think of it as a professional lifetime of development, plateauing, reshaping and growing into your skin as a therapist.

People react differently to the post-qualifying period. This first year out of training can be experienced as either a liberation or a wrench, or shades and mixtures of the two. There is more time to shape your life and consider how to make the next career move. However, there might be elements of being in training which are missed: the regular contact with peers which brings support and companionship on the journey; feeling held within the context of the training group both personally and professionally; having a structured routine for being in college and for study. At deeper levels it may feel like being kicked out of the psychological 'home' and being replaced by the next cohort. As always it is important to acknowledge the complex and ambivalent feelings about the psychological 'home' which trained you.

Elements of transition

Keeping some aspects of what is known whilst moving into the new period helps to maintain some consistency in this post-training year. Continuing to do some work in a familiar placement offers stability and a sense of continuity in this time of transition. The therapist could ask to extend their role, e.g. to start shadowing an assessor, in order to learn these skills or have some mentoring role within the agency – a way of broadening their wings whilst still involved with the placement.

Keeping contact with members of the peer group if and when it is possible is important. Organizing a themed study/discussion day on specific professional topics or a reading day (of all the books you didn't quite manage to read whilst in training) gives a focus for peer meetings. Arranging supervision with peers is also supportive. Sometimes just organizing tea together can feel good.

Supervision – a crucial ingredient

In this transition period and for the rest of professional life, being in supervision is crucial for the continuing development of the therapist. It is also a requirement for membership of the professional organizations. The therapist also needs to be clear about the required amount of supervision demanded by their professional organization. Having good supervision in this post-qualifying period is crucial. There is no longer tutor and group input so a supervisor becomes a key person in the therapist's professional life. I would say choose well rather than choose for convenience at this point in your career.

Further training

Some therapists consider further training after they have qualified. The most usual reason for this is to gain an academic qualification as well as the clinical competency one. So people who have studied on a diploma training course may want to gain a bachelor's or master's degree in counselling or psychotherapy as well. There are also doctoral programmes which experienced therapists with the relevant academic qualifications may wish to consider. In addition, professional organizations – in particular the BACP and the UKCP – want to encourage clinicians to also become researchers in the field to provide data from evidence-based practice.

My opinion is that in the post-qualifying year therapists need to take a breather and that, unless it is of crucial importance to gain a further academic qualification at this point, it is better to wait longer. All the clinical experience which will continue to accumulate in this time will be stored. If at a later date the therapist wants to do an academic or advanced qualification this clinical experience will enhance their understanding of how practice and theory interrelate.

Striking out alone – going into private practice

This is a huge and exciting prospect for most therapists. It can feel like a milestone in their professional life. Having supervision in place for private practice is crucial. Discussions with the supervisor can help not just practically but also to consider the meaning of going into private practice. There are some parallels with starting in training – namely, the issues around time, energy and money.

Self-reflection

Consider the following about starting in private practice:

- *Is it the right time for you?*
- *Do you feel ready and confident enough to go it alone?*
- *What is your motivation for wanting to do it now?*

- *In terms of other facets of your life what would it mean?*
- *What are your hopes and fears for going into private practice?*
- *What is your timescale for building a practice: when would you like it to start?*
- *And how much time do you want it to take up in your life?*

And consider in terms of energy:

- *What else are you committed to in your life?*
- *If you reduced your formal working hours when you were in training, have you increased them again?*
- *If you are still working in a placement setting, how will this impact on your available time?*

Setting up in private practice involves costs – both initial start-up costs and ongoing costs. The major costs include:

1 Room /office space rental. There may be an initial deposit as part of securing the therapy room. Be clear about what a room rental contract demands. For example, does the contract state that the therapist pays for three hours every week for a period of six months regardless of whether the room is in use for all of this time? This is potentially what can make room rental costly, if there are empty appointments. Some renting agencies are flexible whilst others are not. Do some research and calculate the costs, especially costs for 'empty' time in a binding contract. Get a copy of the rental agreement in writing.

2 Working from home. The therapist needs a dedicated space for their professional work which is neutral and not personally orientated. This means there may be costs in transforming a room (or part of a room) into a therapy space, such as decorating and seating arrangements.

3 Advertising. The therapist needs to have a presence on professional websites such as the BACP Find a Therapist site or Counselling Directory or the UKCP website. Costs can also include the setting up of a website which can be linked to the professional directory the therapist is subscribing to. There are also the initial and ongoing costs of having a website.

4 Membership of a professional body. The therapist will now be paying an increased membership fee.

5 Supervision costs.

6 Registering with the Information Commissioner's Office (ICO) – it costs about £40 a year at present (2022).

7 Professional indemnity insurance. The therapist needs malpractice insurance to cover both the legal costs and any successful claim a client may make against them. In deciding what insurance company to use, check how much in cover – especially in terms of legal costs and malpractice cover – the policy will give you.

8 Ongoing continuing professional development (CPD) costs.

Income. It is useful for the therapist to estimate the amount of income they need to live on and to meet the above costs. Have some idea of what non-working time – either through taking a necessary break or through illness – would mean in financial terms. It is unlikely that a therapist would go into a full-time paid therapy post when they qualify. Most therapists have a gradual journey into private practice and earning their living solely as a therapist. In that sense we are like a lot of professionals in the creative industries who have to be adaptable, patient and flexible in order to make it work financially whilst doing the job we trained for and love! Take heart if you are really serious about it and it's right for you: over time clients will find a way to you. There is plenty of need out there!

Taxation on income. Self-employed therapists are responsible for their own fees, accounts and taxes. Some therapists employ an accountant to formally set them up in business and to help them with their annual tax return. Being systematic at keeping records of income and expenditure and keeping receipts and invoices are important administrative tasks around being self-employed. Some therapists do their own tax return. If they do not, seeking an accountant's advice is likely to be valuable, especially if income from therapeutic practice comes from different sources, or if the therapist has income from different sources such as the original 'day job'.

Other practical considerations for setting up

Two aspects of private practice are intrinsically linked together: the therapist's fee structure and how they sell or advertise themselves. There are no set rules about what a therapist can charge in private practice, so deciding on fees is a very personal process. Elements that the therapist needs to consider are:

1 their qualification and level of experience and expertise
2 the costs associated with renting therapy office space or using your home
3 the location of the practice space and what other therapists are charging in the area
4 any particular expertise which gives the therapist specialist knowledge within the field
5 being flexible with fees, e.g. using a sliding scale which takes account of a client's income – if this is offered the therapist needs to decide what would be their lowest fee on the scale.

In effect the therapist is putting a price on their competency, experience, time and talent at this point in their professional career. The fee will certainly be reviewed over the course of their career.

Selling yourself

There is a lot of need for mental health provision but there are a lot of trained therapists too. The therapist has to sell themselves in a competitive market, which may be a personal challenge.

> **Self-reflection – a psychological reflection on my value and experience (as a therapist at this point in my career)**
>
> *Think about what you can offer clients at this point in your career. Get a piece of paper and let yourself write freely, making statements of 'I have ...' and 'I am ...'. Find evidence, or recall feedback from your college tutors, supervisors and peers that you can draw on to build a picture of you as a therapist. Include these comments in your list of attributes.*
>
> *If you like symbols, reread the above list and allow a symbol to emerge which represents what you can offer potential clients. Draw the symbol and if you feel comfortable to continue, imagine holding the symbol in your hand. Then allow yourself to have a sense of its energy and quality. This in symbolic form is what you are offering potential clients. It is important to notice if any gremlins of self-doubt appear when you do this, as these indicate there is something within you that could still undermine your sense of professional self.*

All advertising literature requires that the therapist lists their qualifications and membership of professional organizations. However, the therapist has to advertise themselves as a practitioner and a person, and to convey to the public what is at the heart of their clinical practice. Work this out and make it as human as possible. Prospective clients on the whole do not want to be blinded by science or elaborate psychological language and terms. They want to know the therapist is qualified, but above that they want a person who they can talk to at this time of trouble or distress in their lives.

Boundaries and fees

The main clinical difference between being in training and working in private practice is that you will be doing the screening and assessment of potential clients.

When I started in clinical practice a potential client would ring me up to make an initial appointment so I got to hear their voice and this gave me a sense of the person. Nowadays many initial appointments are made solely through email communication. This is convenient in many ways but it means the therapist has no feel for the person who will be arriving at their door or in their online room. This may seem less important if the therapist is working online or in a practice with other practitioners. But in private practice at home with no-one else around this may not feel as safe for a new therapist. One way of increasing a sense of personal safety is for therapists to set up an initial assessment meeting at home when they know someone else is around. This is not intended to be alarmist but it is a caution to take note of if the therapist lives and works alone and has not much experience with new clients in their own space. It is a reason some therapists never work in their own home.

The other main difference is that the money is a direct payment for the therapist's professional expertise. If a client doesn't pay it will have a financial impact upon the therapist. Being clear and transparent about the fee structure before the first meeting is part of making a contract with the client, and an ethical action. I remember a trainee telling me she was going to meet a therapist but the therapist had not told her what the fee was, so the trainee went to the meeting with a wad of cash. This is not really acceptable and it creates anxiety in the potential client.

Another part of this 'money' talk centres around clarity about payment – how and when you want to be paid, e.g. on the day of the session, before the session or at the end of the month after you have submitted an invoice (which states the time period to make the payment), and the method of payment, e.g. electronic payment, cash or cheque (very rare now!). Additionally, make the cancellations policy clear – i.e. when can a client cancel before they are charged a cancellation fee? Probably one of the most difficult discussions about money arises when a client pays late, forgets their money or goes into arrears with their fees. This is a test of the therapist's sense of what is due to themselves as a practitioner and how they can challenge this behaviour, which is also very relevant to the therapeutic relationship.

Some therapists choose to make a written agreement with the client before the first session or during the first session, which sets out the main aspects of their business and ethical contract with their client. Money (business) is a key component of this contract.

Clinical responsibility – making an assessment

There are many ways to make a clinical assessment, ranging from a very open question such as 'This space is for you. Can you tell me about yourself and why you have come?' to having some key points that the therapist wants to know about a client, to a structured assessment form with specific questions. I suggest having some kind of intake form is helpful as a newly qualified therapist. It will provide a framework to base this first meeting around, which is supportive. It will also give a general sense of the client's story and help the therapist decide (maybe with the assistance of a supervisor) if the client's story and issues are within the therapist's competency to work with. Making an assessment is not a 100 per cent indicator that there will be a good therapeutic match forever, because material can emerge during the therapeutic process that sheds a different light on the client and what they need. However, this initial assessment is an important opportunity for the therapist to decide if it is appropriate to offer a therapeutic contract to the client.

In making an assessment, finding out what I call the '4 Ps and 1 M' of the client's life gives some core information which helps in deciding whether to offer to work with a client or not. The 4 Ps encompass information about the client's past, their present situation, their presenting issue and the people in the client's life and in their head. The M stands for their motivation to work on themselves.

The past. You need to know something of the client's past – to know about their roots, family background and relationships, their experience of education, their culture, their sense of identity including sexual identity through their life, any history of addiction and recovery which they have been through, and any other key events in their working or personal life, e.g. loss, success stories, problems or failures that they deem significant. In forming a picture of the client's past it's not about bombarding them with questions all the way through but inviting them to share what they can about the past which will have had an influence on shaping them. Listen out too for what they don't say. If the client says 'I had a wonderful childhood' and then cannot relate anything in detail about what made it wonderful or about how they related to key figures in their early life, this is probably significant. Maintaining and responding empathically throughout this information-gathering process is an art in itself – not to mention being able to write this information down (or type) whilst maintaining contact with the client. This is where a structured form may help in the early days.

The present. The therapist needs to know about the client's present circumstances to have a sense of what is holding them, supporting them and keeping them safe and connected to ordinary life processes and functions; what their resources and interests are that will sustain them on the journey of exploration. Therapy can disturb. Getting a sense of their solid ground and resources in the present or the positive factors in their current life is important.

The presenting issue. Why has the client come to seek help – what is the ostensible reason why they are there? Can the client actually explain what they want? Also, what is significant about the timing of seeking help? Has something triggered their cry for help, has there been a build-up of problems, has a crisis emerged or has someone encouraged or pushed them into seeking help? Very rarely does a client come merely for the purpose of wanting to know themselves better.

People in the client's life. Being interested in the key people in the client's life both past and present is important. If the client can describe some reliable and supportive people and relationships this will assist the creation of the therapeutic relationship at the start. If the client has experienced a series of poor professional therapeutic relationships this is likely to set off the present therapy on the wrong foot because of the transference dynamics. Good relationships in the present will act to help the therapy progress. A history of poor relationships, especially if there has been betrayal or abuse of trust, lack of support or other malignant responses to the client, can initially act against the therapist and against the therapy itself.

In addition, there are the people who live within the client's own head – the internal voices that tell them not to trust, to sort it out themselves, to get on with it – otherwise the therapy will never work. Or the client may be so busy acting out elements of the Drama Triangle (Karpman 1968) that they don't work collaboratively with the therapist in their own best interests.

Motivation. When a client wants to be in therapy, has some degree of hope that the therapist will be able to help them, is willing to engage and think about themselves and has some desire to be different, these are encouraging signs for the work. If a client is very anxious in this first meeting this may conceal their underlying motivation for being in therapy, until their anxiety decreases as trust builds between the two therapeutic partners. Clients who want other people to change and have no capacity to think about their own part in the drama of their lives are in what Prochaska and Di Clemente (1983) call the pre-contemplation state, which makes starting in therapy challenging.

Meeting the client and making an assessment in the first session, or over a series of three to six sessions, is important for laying the foundation for the therapeutic relationship. It is sometimes difficult to make a decision whether to offer a client therapy after one meeting.

A way around this is to see the first contract of six sessions as an extended assessment period. It will give the chance to see if continuing to work together is appropriate. The client may also have reservations. If the therapist senses the client is not sure about saying 'yes' to therapy at the end of the assessment, invite them to think about it for a week and then to confirm whether they wish to start in therapy or not.

Designing your own form

Here are some things to consider when designing an intake form. Look at the form the placement uses and decide what is useful in it and what to add to or subtract from it. Even in this digital age where a lot of contact is made by mobile or email I consider basic details such as the client's address and date of birth are important to make a note of. What is more controversial is whether to ask for the name of the client's GP practice for emergency situations. Personally I think it's wise to have this information at hand. If a client is concerned about this you can explain its purpose, which will then ensure a discussion about the boundaries of confidentiality and the exceptions to it. Having an online practice it is prudent to have an emergency contact person for the client in case of a sudden event during the session, e.g. the client faints.

Below is a table with the key themes for information and discussion with the client in order to gain an overall picture of the client's life and their present situation. The skill is in settling the client into the session and building a rapport with them. Be open and let the client know that notes will be taken which are protected as confidential and ask them if they are agreeable to this. Then start with the basic factual details. It helps the settling in process. After this enquire about the client's family background and early life. I usually let a client say what they want to say and notice what they might omit. Sometimes I might follow up such omissions with a gentle enquiry but I do not probe.

The table below identifies the key themes in clinical assessment and the details to build questions around.

1	Basic details: • phone/mobile • email address • home address • emergency contact number • name of GP surgery
2	Family background: • birthplace of client • family background – where the family comes from • members of the family and the client's position within the family
3	Key family relationships: • relationships with parents/key caregivers • relationships with siblings • relationships with other significant family members
4	Education: • how was it? • further education or not? • impact on the client's sense of identity
5	Significant relationships: • when young • in adulthood • in the present • recurring patterns of relationship
6	Work and purpose: • work and career history • ongoing purpose in life • current situation
7	Health and mental health history: • significant illnesses in life • any current illness and treatment • history of mental illness including treatment or psychological intervention • was treatment helpful? • suicidal ideation or attempts – past or present • risk factors in the client's present
8	Attitude to life: • what is it? • what has been meaningful in their life? • what are the challenges?
9	Current life circumstances: • living arrangements • daily routine

10	Sense of self: • sense of identity • gender and sexual identity • relationship with own body, feelings and thoughts • how much at home in their own skin?
11	Any additional questions arising from replies to the above questions: • anything else significant that the client wants to add
12	Purpose: • why have they come to therapy? • why now – what triggered it? • what do they hope to gain? • any fears or concerns about you or being in therapy?

Care of self in the early years

Unless the therapist has a job in an organization they will be a sole practitioner and left to their own devices to create a structure for their work/life balance. A big challenge in the quest to build a practice and have an income (if you do not have another source of income) is structuring working hours and planning appropriate breaks from the work. It's good to start with making a timetable to map out a working plan for the week. Note: this is not set in stone.

Self-reflection

- *When do you want to work? Identify specific times in the week. It's best to see this as blocks of time, e.g. Monday between 5 and 8 pm.*
- *How many clients are you able to see, or would you like to see, within these time blocks?*
- *How willing are you to work in the evenings and if so how many evenings?*
- *Do you want to work at weekends?*

The time blocks when they will be working may be determined by the rented space the therapist uses. If working from home, the therapist may think it's easier to see clients when it's convenient for them. This open availability doesn't usually work in the long term for the therapist, as the work becomes fragmented and spread over too wide a time period. This is particularly so when offering evening appointments. One client each evening of the week does not afford regular free evening space for a private life. So start by being clear about what blocks of time will be dedicated working hours. Whatever is decided is not written in stone and can be readjusted: our lives change and our needs change. Taking time to review if the timetable suits you is important so that your own well-being is maintained.

Another element in structuring a work schedule is to deliberately include breaks. In the early days if client work is the sole source of income it is tempting to keep going week after week. We need breaks and clearly defined spaces in our life away from work even when we love what we are doing and it's going well. By putting definite breaks/holiday times into a calendar well in advance there is something to look forward to and there will be time to let clients know that there will be a break in the future. Short breaks are good, but longer breaks from work allow more time for rest and recharging the batteries. It became apparent when working with one of my supervisees that he did not plan breaks into his year, resulting in a kind of relentless grind which had to be challenged. It is very difficult to do this in private practice because a break does mean no income over that period of time. However, not taking appropriate breaks can affect the therapist's stamina and their ability to concentrate on the work.

Once a private practice has developed, the therapist will be working with a larger number of clients than in training. It gives great joy to be achieving this cherished professional aim. However, there may be a greater impact on the therapist in terms of the amount of subtle energies being absorbed through the work. On the one hand, the therapist is more experienced and better able to psychologically cleanse themselves. However, the larger number of clients, and their conscious and unconscious psychological processes, will have an impact on the therapist at some level. This is an ongoing aspect of the work but new therapists tend to discount it in their enthusiasm for practising professionally. If the therapist has chosen to be without therapy they may not realize that they have a build-up of psychological residue and perhaps undischarged stress. Developing a good reflective habit by considering 'What is still stuck in me?' is a useful care-of-self question. On a daily level, sitting with clients and sitting whilst working online means immobility. Fitting in some kind of physical exercise is helpful. Going for short walks during gaps between clients is one solution.

Most people who work in private practice work largely in isolation. If the therapist works in a centre or in therapy rooms there may be other colleagues around, and it's a good idea to establish friendly links with them. If the therapist works at home it's important to think about what outside contact could be enhancing. It's great to be your own boss but we all need regular and nourishing contact with others. It can be lonely being a sole practitioner.

Away from the training environment which provided stimulus and connection there is a need to find other sources of professional development, psychological and spiritual nourishment. Therapists in their listening capacity are performing the complex processes of holding, containing and regulating another person's ideas as well as giving deeply of themselves through their presence in the room. Think beyond the obligatory continuing professional development (CPD) which is required, and continue with practices and activities that give a sense of life, interest, joy and well-being. Exploring something new also brings fresh energy into your personal life. We need mental and spiritual nourishment in order to do the work we do. If we are seriously deprived of it for long periods of time there is the danger of burnout. This is both personally damaging and also puts in jeopardy the new career which has been built up. The trick is to be vigilant so that a build-up of exhaustion does not happen.

The early years of practice and beyond

The post-qualifying year is really a year of consolidating clinical practice and considering if it's the right time to set up in private practice. Having settled into the work after training the therapist will discover what themes and areas of work they prefer working with and recognize areas of expertise that they wish to develop further. This is something to consider throughout a working life; however, it is also good to think about what to develop in the next two to five years. Making professional goals or plans can increase the motivation to keep developing as a clinician and will steer the therapist towards CPD events or further training.

Something to notice – and it's completely normal – is that at some time in the early years of practice the initial elation about doing the work becomes less intense. The therapist develops a more routine attitude to doing the work. There are probably fewer highs and fewer anxious or dispiriting lows. In essence, the therapist has grown into a more steady professional position. This is a sign of being well embedded in the profession and quietly identifying with a new professional role.

Our own journey of life continues alongside this professional development and will in some ways influence it. This is a profession where there is no absolute boundary between our professional and personal psyches. We need to be aware of both. Hopefully one is enriched by the other, and when difficult times come the learnings we gain permeate into our core selves and can be used both personally and for the deeper understanding of our clients. As the journey continues over the years of practice, the deep joy and commitment to listening to clients will also continue.

Bibliography

Adoption and Children Act (2002) Available at https://www.legislation.gov.uk/ukpga/2002/38/contents (accessed 18 November 2022).

Alyn, J.H. (1988) The politics of touch in therapy: A response to Willison and Masson, *Journal of Counselling and Development*, 66(9): 432–3.

Assagioli, R. (1965) *Psychosynthesis*. Wellingborough: Turnstone Press.

Banaji, M.R. and Greenwald, A.G. (2013) *Blind Spot: Hidden Biases of Good People*. New York: Delacorte Press.

Berne, E. (1961) *Transactional Analysis in Psychotherapy*. New York: Grove Press.

Black, P. and Wiliam, D. (1998) Assessment and classroom learning, *Assessment in Education: Principles, Policy & Practice*, 5(1): 7–74.

Bordin, E.S. (1979) The generalizability of the psychoanalytical concept of the working alliance. *Psychotherapy: Theory, Research and Practice*, 16(3): 252–260.

Bowlby, J. (1969) *Attachment and Loss*, Volume 1: *Attachment*. London: Hogarth Press.

British Association for Counselling and Psychotherapy (BACP) (2018) BACP Ethical Framework for the Counselling Professions. Available at https://www.bacp.co.uk/events-and-resources/ethics-and-standards/ethical-framework-for-the-counselling-professions/ (accessed 28 November 2022).

Carroll, M. and Tholstrup, M. (eds) (2001) *Integrative Approaches to Supervision*. London: Jessica Kingsley.

Casement, P. (1985) *On Learning From the Patient*. London: Tavistock.

Children Act (2004) Available at https://www.legislation.gov.uk/ukpga/2004/31/contents (accessed 18 November 2022).

Clance, P.R. and Imes, S.A. (1978) The imposter phenomenon in high achieving women: Dynamics and therapeutic intervention, *Psychotherapy: Theory, Research & Practice*, 15(3): 241–7.

Clarkson, P. (1987) The bystander role, *Transactional Analysis Journal*, 17(3): 82–7.

Clarkson, P. (1993) *On Psychotherapy*. London: Whurr Publishers.

Cooper, M. (2008) *Essential Research Findings in Counselling and Psychotherapy*. London: SAGE Publications.

CORE OM (n.d.) Company home page. Available at https://www.corc.uk.net/media/1326/201511learning_from_core_measurement.pdf (accessed 28 November 2022).

Culley, S. (1991) *Integrative Counselling Skills in Action*. London: SAGE Publications.

Cutcliffe, J.R., Butterworth, T. and Proctor, B. (eds) (2001) *Fundamental Themes in Clinical Supervision*. London: Routledge.

DiAngelo, R. (2018) *White Fragility: Why It's So Hard for White People to Talk About Racism*. Boston, MA: Beacon Press.

Dottolo, A. and Kaschak, E. (eds) (2016) *Whiteness and White Privilege in Psychotherapy*. London: Routledge.

Fisher, J. (2017) *Healing the Fragmented Selves of Trauma Survivors*. London: Routledge.

Ginot, E. (2007) Intersubjectivity and neuroscience: Understanding enactments and their significance in emerging paradigms, *Psychoanalytic Psychology*, 24(2): 317–32.

Gomez, L. (1997) *An Introduction to Object Relations*. London: Free Association Books.

Hawkins, P. (1985) Humanistic psychotherapy supervision: A conceptual framework, *Self and Society: Journal of Humanistic Psychology*, 13(2): 69–79.

Hawkins, P. and Shohet, R. (2006) *Supervision in the Helping Professions*. Maidenhead: Open University Press.

Herman, J. (2001) *Trauma and Recovery*. London: Pandora.

Hill Collins, P. and Bilge, S. (2016) *Intersectionality*. Cambridge: Polity Press.

Hitchcock, S. (2022) If adoption comes up with an existing client, do we always need to refer them to an Ofsted registered counsellor?, *Therapy Today*, 33(3): 50–1.

Holmes, J. (1993) *John Bowlby & Attachment Theory*. London: Routledge.

Horton, J.A., Clance, P.R., Sterk-Elifson, C. and Emshoff, J. (1995) Touch in psychotherapy: A survey of patients' experiences, *Psychotherapy*, 32(3): 443–57.

Horvath, A.O. and Bedi, R.P. (2002) The alliance, in John C. Norcross (ed.) *Psychotherapy Relationships that Work: Therapist Contributions and Responsiveness to Patients*. New York: Oxford University Press, pp. 37–69.

Howard, S. (2010) *Skills in Psychodynamic Counselling and Psychotherapy*. London: SAGE Publications.

Hycner, R. (1993) *Between Person and Person*. Highland, NY: Gestalt Journal Press.

Jacobs, M. (2003) Colleagues or Opponents (CSCT Forum), Colleagues or Opponents – YouTube. Available at https://www.youtube.com/watch?v=LFlr0GmrGho (accessed 18 November 2022).

Jenkins, P. (2007) *Counselling, Psychotherapy and the Law*. London: SAGE Publications.

Karpman, S. (1968) Fairy tales and script drama analysis, *Transactional Analysis Bulletin*, 7(26): 39–43.

Klein, M. (1988) *Envy and Gratitude and Other Works 1946–1963*. London: Virago Press.

Kroenke, K., Spitzer, R.L. and Williams, J.B. (2001) The PHQ-9: Validity of a brief depression severity measure, *Journal of General Internal Medicine*, 16(9): 606–13.

Kübler-Ross, E. (1969) *On Death and Dying*. London: Tavistock.

Luft, J. and Ingham, H. (1955) The Johari window, a graphic model of interpersonal awareness, in *Proceedings of the Western Training Laboratory in Group Development*. Los Angeles, CA: University of California.

Maroda, K. (2010) *Psychodynamic Techniques*. New York: Guilford Press.

Mitchels, B. and Bond, T. (2010) *Essential Law for Counsellors and Psychotherapists*. London: SAGE Publications.

Mollon, P. (2002) *Shame and Jealousy*. London: Karnac.

Norcross, C. and Goldfried, M.R. (eds) (1992) *Handbook of Psychotherapy Integration*. New York: Basic Books.

O'Brien, M. and Houston, G. (2000) *Integrative Counselling*. London: SAGE Publications.

Ofsted (2021) Introduction to Adoption Support Agencies (Guidance). Available at https://www.gov.uk/government/publications/adoption-support-agencies-introduction-to-registration/introduction-to-adoption-support-agencies (accessed 18 November 2022).

Orlinsky, D.E., Grawe, K. and Parks, B. (1994) Process and outcome in psychotherapy – Noch einmal, in A.E. Bergin and S.L. Garfield (eds) *Handbook of Psychotherapy and Behaviour Change*. New York: John Wiley, pp. 270–376.

Prevent duty guidance (2015) Available at https://www.legislation.gov.uk/ukdsi/2015/9780111133309/pdfs/ukdsiod_9780111133309_en.pdf (accessed 18 November 2022).

Prevention of Terrorism Act (2005) Available at https://www.legislation.gov.uk/ukpga/2005/2/contents (accessed 18 November 2022).

Prochaska, J.O. and Di Clemente, C.C. (1983) Stages and processes of self-change of smoking: Toward an integrative model of change, *Journal of Consulting and Clinical Psychology*, 51(3): 390–5.

Proctor, B. (1987) Supervision: A co-operative exercise in accountability, in M. Marken and M. Payne (eds) *Enabling and Ensuring*. Leicester: Leicester National Youth Bureau and Council for Education and Training in Youth and Community Work, pp. 21–3.

Proctor, G. (2017) *The Dynamics of Power in Counselling and Psychotherapy: Ethics, Politics and Practice*, 2nd edn. Monmouth: PCCS Books.

Rogers, C.R. (1957) The necessary and sufficient conditions of personality change, *Journal Consulting Clinical Psychology*, 21(2): 95–103.

Rogers, C.R. (1967) *On Becoming a Person*. London: Constable.

Rogers, C.R. (2007) The necessary and sufficient conditions of therapeutic personality change, *Psychotherapy: Theory, Research, Practice, Training*, 44(3): 240–8.

Rowan, J. and Jacobs, M. (2002) *The Therapist's Use of Self*. Buckingham: Open University Press.

Rycroft, C. (1995) *A Critical Dictionary of Psychoanalysis*, 2nd edn. London: Penguin.

Safran, J.D., Crocker, P., McMain, S. and Murray, P. (1990) Therapeutic alliance rupture as a therapy event for empirical investigation, *Psychotherapy: Theory, Research, Practice, Training*, 27(2): 154–65.

Schore, A.N. (2012) *The Science of the Art of Psychotherapy*. New York: W.W. Norton.

SCoPEd Framework (2022) Available at https://www.bacp.co.uk/media/14435/scoped-framework-january-2022.pdf (accessed 18 November 2022).

Searles, H.F. (1955) The informational value of the supervisor's emotional experience, in *Collected Papers of Schizophrenia and Related Subjects*. London: Hogarth Press.

Sexual Offences Act (2003) Available at https://www.legislation.gov.uk/ukpga/2003/42/contents (accessed 18 November 2022).

Siegel, D.J. (1999) *The Developing Mind: Toward a Neurobiology of Interpersonal Experience*. New York: Guilford Press.

Siegel, D.J. (2010) *The Mindful Therapist*. New York: W.W. Norton.

Smith, E.W.L., Clance, P.R. and Imes, S. (eds) (1998) *Touch in Psychotherapy: Theory, Research, and Practice*. New York: Guilford Press.

Spitzer, R.L., Kroenke, K., Williams, J.B. and Löwe, B. (2006) A brief measure for assessing generalized anxiety disorder: The GAD-7, *Archives of Internal Medicine*, 166(10): 1092–7.

Stern, D. (1985) *The Interpersonal World of the Infant*. New York: Basic Books.

Stewart, I. and Joines, V. (2012) *TA Today: A New Introduction to Transactional Analysis*, 2nd edn. Chapel Hill, NC: Lifespan Publishing.

Stoltenberg, C. and Delworth, U. (1987) *Supervising Counsellors and Therapists: A Developmental Approach*. San Francisco, CA: Jossey-Bass Wiley.

Stroebe, M. and Schut, H. (1999) The dual process model of coping with bereavement: Rationale and description, *Death Studies*, 23(3): 197–224.

Sussman, M.B. (1992) *A Curious Calling*. Northvale, NJ: Jason Aronson.

The Data Protection Act (2018) Available at https://www.gov.uk/data-protection (accessed 18 November 2022).

The Glossary of Education Reform (2015) Available at https://www.edglossary.org/assessment/ (accessed 18 November 2022).

The Protection of Children and Vulnerable Adults and Care Standards Tribunal regulations (2002) Available at https://www.legislation.gov.uk/uksi/2002/816/contents/made (accessed 18 November 2022).

Tuckman, B.W. (1965) Developmental sequence in small groups, *Psychological Bulletin*, 63(6): 384–99.

Tuckman, B.W. and Jensen, M.A. (1977) Stages of small-group development revisited, *Group & Organization Studies*, 2(4): 419–27.

Turner, D. (2021) *Intersections of Privilege and Otherness in Counselling and Psychotherapy: Mockingbird*. London: Routledge.

UKCP (2019*) UKCP Code of Ethics and Professional Standards*. Available at https://www.psychotherapy.org.uk/media/bkjdm33f/ukcp-code-of-ethics-and-professional-practice-2019.pdf (accessed 28 November 2022).

Wallin, D.J. (2007) *Attachment in Psychotherapy*. New York: Guilford Press.

Ware, P. (1983) Personality adaptations, *Transactional Analysis Journal*, 13(1): 11–19.

Winnicott, D.W. (1990) *The Maturational Processes and the Facilitating Environment*. London: Karnac.

Worden, J.W. (1991) *Grief Counselling and Grief Therapy*, 2nd edn. London: Routledge.

Woskett, V. and Page, S. (2001) *Supervising the Counsellor: A Cyclical Model*. London: Routledge.

Index